ns

Science

Key Stage 2

Revision Guide

Penny Johnson

Introduction

The purpose of this book

This book will help you to revise for the science tests at the end of Year 6 and to get better marks in them.

What you will need

Paper, graph paper, a ruler and a pencil or pen.

How to use this book

- It is best to start at the beginning and work through each topic in turn. If you prefer, you could use the Contents List or the Index to choose a topic.
- Turn to the topic and read the explanation.
- Some of the words in each topic appear in orange. Their definitions are given in the Glossary on pages 94 and 95. Other important words are in **bold**. Try to remember them.
- The **Remember** section at the end of the topic lists the most important things you need to know. Read it through, then cover it up. Can you remember what it says?
- Try the **Test yourself!** questions. Some of the questions are more difficult and these are printed with a star (★) next to them. Write your answers on a piece of paper. Then check them against the correct answers on pages 88 to 91.
- Maybe you got some questions wrong, or perhaps you're not sure that you understand the topic? Read it again and have another go at the questions.
- If you get a good mark and are sure that you understand, tick the circle in the corner of the page, and move on.
- When you have worked through the whole book, check whether there is a tick for every topic. Are any circles empty? If so, you need to go back to those topics and work through them again.
- Read the 'Tips for tests' at the back of this book. Then you are ready to take the tests. Good luck!

How to get even better marks!

- Work through the Schofield & Sims Science Practice Papers for Key Stage 2, available separately.

Note for teachers and parents

The Schofield & Sims Revision Guides have been written by teachers, for use at school and at home. The Guides enable children to revise independently for the National Curriculum Key Stage tests (SATs). The focus is on clear explanations of the topics covered by the tests, all of which will already have been taught in school. Each science topic is matched to the Science National Curriculum, and all the curricular links are listed in the Curriculum chart on pages 92 to 93. Practice Papers designed to accompany this book will help to further improve children's test results (see back cover for full details).

Contents

What is science?

Science is a way of finding out about the things around us.

Scientists investigate living things. They find out:

- how our bodies work
- how plants grow
- where different plants and animals live, and what they feed on
- how to keep healthy.

You can find out more about these things on pages 5 to 33.

Scientists investigate materials. They find out:

- about the **properties** of different materials
- about the rocks and **soil**
- what happens when you heat things up and cool them down
- how you can mix materials together and then separate them again
- what happens when new materials are made.

You can find out more about these things on pages 34 to 59.

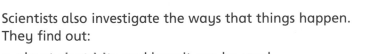

Scientists also investigate the ways that things happen. They find out:

- about **electricity** and how it can be used
- about different kinds of forces, and what they can do
- how we see and hear things
- about the Earth, and why we have **day** and **night**.

You can find out more about these things on pages 60 to 80.

You need to learn some of the things that scientists have already found out about the world around us, but you also need to learn how to investigate things for yourself. You can learn some of the skills you need for investigations on pages 81 to 87.

Living things

You are a human being and you are alive. You need to eat food to stay alive.

Humans are animals, and all animals need to eat.

The scientific word for eating food is **nutrition**. Nutrition is a life process. It is something that all living things do.

Here are five life processes that all living things do.

Nutrition	Animals get their food by eating plants or other animals. Plants make their own food using sunlight.
Respiration	Animals and plants need oxygen to help them to use their food.
Movement	Animals need to move to find food. Plants do not move around like animals, but they can move parts of themselves: • sunflowers can turn to face the Sun • some flowers close up at night.
Growth	Animals are very small when they are born. They grow bigger and bigger until they are adults. Plants also grow. A tiny seed can grow into a huge tree.
Reproduction	Animals **reproduce** when they make new animals like themselves. Plants reproduce by making **seeds**. New plants grow from the seeds.

Test yourself!

1 Write down the names of five life processes.
2 How do animals get their food?
3 How do plants get their food?
4 How do plants reproduce?

Remember

All living things have **life processes**.

Nutrition means **using food to stay alive**.

Through **respiration**, living things use oxygen to help them to use their food.

All living things **move** and **grow**.

Reproduction means **making new living things**.

Teeth

You need teeth to help you to eat. Your food needs to be cut into small pieces and chewed before you swallow it.

Your teeth have different shapes to do different jobs.

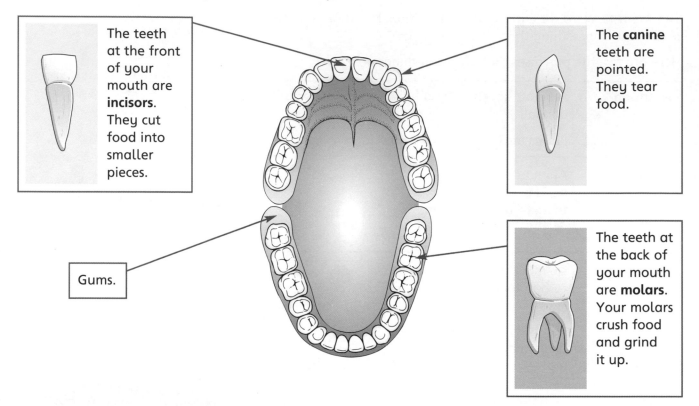

The teeth at the front of your mouth are **incisors**. They cut food into smaller pieces.

The **canine** teeth are pointed. They tear food.

Gums.

The teeth at the back of your mouth are **molars**. Your molars crush food and grind it up.

What kinds of teeth do animals have?

Animals have different shaped teeth, depending on what they eat. Horses eat grass, so they have bigger molars to help them to grind up the grass. Dogs eat other animals. Their teeth help them to kill and eat their food.

Some of the molars are pointed to cut up meat.

The canine teeth are very long to help dogs to kill other animals.

Some animals do not have teeth. Birds have beaks instead of teeth, and animals like worms do not have any hard parts in their mouths at all!

Looking after your teeth

When you were born you didn't have any teeth. Your first teeth are your **milk teeth**. They started to grow when you were about six months old. A new set of teeth grows under your milk teeth, and your milk teeth start to fall out when you are about six years old. These new teeth are your **permanent teeth**.

You need to look after your teeth and gums. Bits of food or sugar stay in your mouth after you eat or drink. These can make your teeth decay. If a tooth decays very badly it may fall out, or it may have to be taken out by a dentist.

It is very important to look after your permanent teeth. If one of your permanent teeth comes out, you cannot grow a new one to take its place!

How to look after your teeth

- brush them twice a day – once after breakfast, and once just before you go to bed at night

- don't eat sweets or foods with sugar in

- avoid fizzy drinks

- choose foods like apples and carrots, and drinks like milk – all these can help to keep your teeth healthy

- go to the dentist for a check-up – if you have any decay, the dentist can give you a filling to stop it getting any worse.

Test yourself!

1 Why do humans need teeth?

2 What are the three kinds of teeth called?

3 Why do horses have big molar teeth?

4 What are your milk teeth?

5 Write down five ways of looking after your teeth.

★6 Lions eat meat. What do you think lions' teeth are like? Explain your answer.

Remember

Teeth help you to **cut your food** into small pieces before you swallow it.

Incisors cut food into **smaller pieces**.

Canines tear up food.

Molars crush and grind up food.

Other animals have **different teeth**, depending on **what they eat**.

Humans have **two sets of teeth: milk teeth** and **permanent teeth**.

You can **keep your teeth and gums healthy** by **brushing** them, and by **not eating sugary food**.

A healthy diet

Your **diet** is all the different kinds of food that you eat each day.

You need food:
- to help you to grow
- to keep your body healthy
- to give you energy to move around.

You need different foods to help your body to do all of these things.

Foods to help you to grow

- Meat and fish

- Milk, cheese and eggs

- Beans and lentils

Foods to keep your body healthy

- Fruit

- Vegetables

Foods to give you energy

- Bread, pasta, rice and cereals contain **starch**.

  CORN FLAKES

  RICE

- Milk, cheese, butter, cooking oil and meat contain **fats** and **oils**. You should not eat too much of these foods.

  Olive Oil

- Sweets, cakes, biscuits and fizzy drinks contain **sugar**. You should not eat too much of these foods.

  COLA

What is a balanced diet?

A diet that has the right **mixture** of different foods to give your body all that it needs is called a **balanced diet**.

You need:

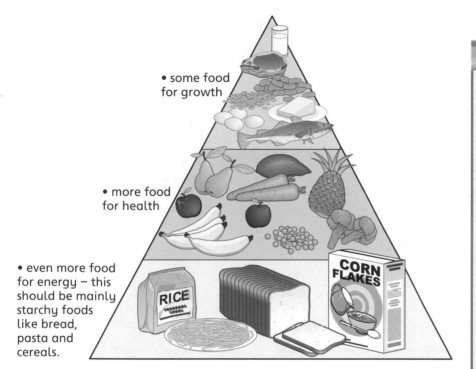

- some food for growth

- more food for health

- even more food for energy – this should be mainly starchy foods like bread, pasta and cereals.

Test yourself!

1 Write down three reasons why your body needs food.

2 Which foods help your body to grow?

3 Which foods give you energy?

4 Which foods keep your body healthy?

5 What is a balanced diet?

★6 Sue eats fish and chips at lunchtime, and has a burger in a bun for tea. Explain to Sue how and why she should change her diet.

There are lots of different ways of getting a balanced diet! These meals all give you the foods your body needs.

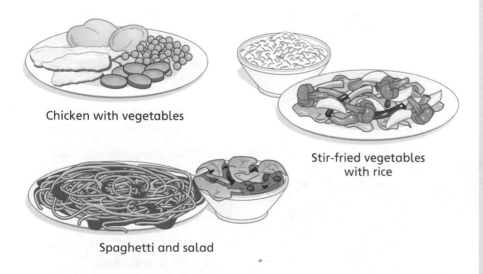

Chicken with vegetables

Stir-fried vegetables with rice

Spaghetti and salad

Animals also need healthy diets. Different animals need different diets. For instance, rabbits need to eat a lot of leaves and vegetables such as carrots. Cats need to eat a lot of meat.

Remember

A **healthy diet** gives you food for **growth**, for **energy**, and to **keep your body healthy**.

Meat, **fish**, **eggs**, **milk**, **cheese**, **beans** and **lentils** help you to **grow**.

Bread, **pasta**, **rice** and **cereals** give you **energy**.

Fruit and **vegetables** keep your body **healthy**.

A **balanced diet** gives your body **all the different kinds of foods** that it needs.

Skeletons

You have a **skeleton** inside your body. Your skeleton is made of lots of different bones. Your bones were very small when you were born, and they got bigger as you grew bigger.

Your skeleton does three jobs:

- it protects parts of your body
- it supports your body (you couldn't stand up without your skeleton!)
- it lets you move.

Your **ribs** protect your **heart** and lungs.

Your **skull** protects your brain.

Your **spine** is sometimes called your backbone. Your spine supports your body.

Joints let your arms and legs bend.

Do other animals have skeletons?

Many other animals have skeletons. All animals that have a spine are called **vertebrates**.

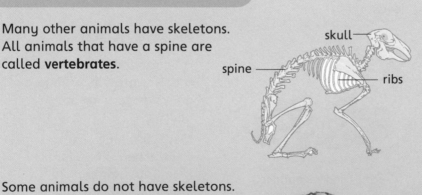

skull

spine

ribs

Some animals do not have skeletons.

Animals like crabs have hard parts outside their bodies.

Animals like worms do not have hard parts at all.

Test yourself!

1 Write down three reasons why you need a skeleton.

2 What does your skull do?

3 How does your skeleton allow you to move?

Remember

Your **skeleton protects** and **supports** your body, and allows you to **move**.

Not all animals have a skeleton.

Muscles

The joints in your **skeleton** let your body move, but your bones cannot move on their own! You need **muscles** to move your arms and legs.

Muscles pull on your bones to move your body. When a muscle pulls, it **contracts** (gets shorter).

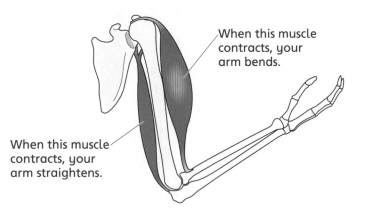

When this muscle contracts, your arm bends.

When this muscle contracts, your arm straightens.

Your muscles can only pull on bones. They cannot push. This means that your muscles have to work in pairs. When one muscle is contracting, the other is **relaxing** (getting longer).

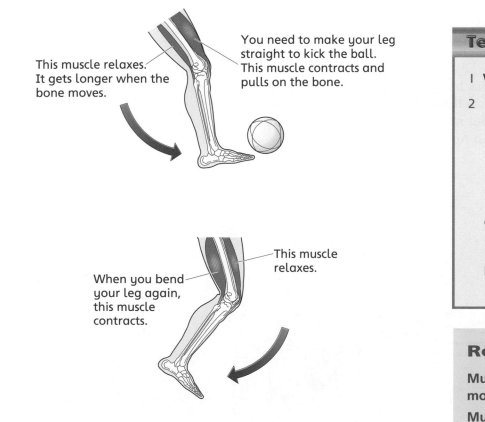

This muscle relaxes. It gets longer when the bone moves.

You need to make your leg straight to kick the ball. This muscle contracts and pulls on the bone.

This muscle relaxes.

When you bend your leg again, this muscle contracts.

Some muscles in your body do not make bones move. You have lots of muscles in your face, which can make you frown or smile, or blink your eyes.

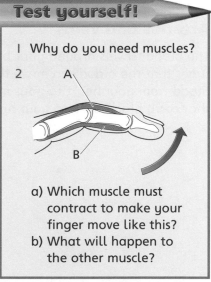

Test yourself!

1 Why do you need muscles?

2 A

   B

a) Which muscle must contract to make your finger move like this?
b) What will happen to the other muscle?

Remember

Muscles make your body **move**.

Muscles can only **pull**; they **cannot push**.

Muscles work in **pairs**.

Your heart

When you run around or play games you breathe faster, you get hot, and you might feel tired. Sometimes you can also feel your **heart** beating faster. This means that your heart is getting oxygen to the **muscles** more quickly than usual, because they have been working hard.

Your muscles need food to keep them working. Food, oxygen and other substances are carried around your body in **blood**. Your heart pumps blood around your body.

Your heart is in your chest, and it is protected by your **ribs**.

The walls of your heart are made of muscle. There are spaces inside it that are filled with blood. The heart muscle **contracts** (gets smaller) and squeezes blood out. This pumps blood around your body.

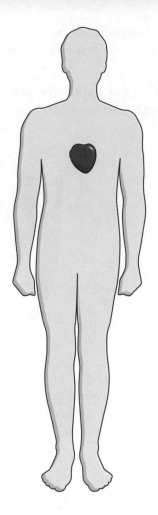

Arteries and veins

The blood travels around your body in **blood vessels**. These are tubes that the blood can move through. The blood vessels that carry blood from your heart to your muscles are called **arteries**. The ones that carry blood back to your heart are called **veins**.

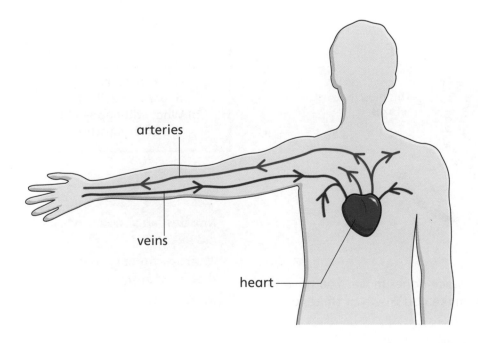

arteries

veins

heart

What is your pulse?

You can feel the blood moving through your **blood vessels** in your neck or in your wrist. The movements you can feel are called your **pulse**. Each beat of your pulse is made by one beat of your heart. Your **pulse rate** is the number of beats per minute. Your pulse rate depends on what you are doing.

When you run around your muscles need more food. This means that more blood has to flow to your muscles, so your heart has to beat faster. When you stop running around, it takes a little while for your pulse rate to go down to its normal level again.

How does exercise affect your pulse rate?

The graph below shows what happened to Danny's heart rate during break.

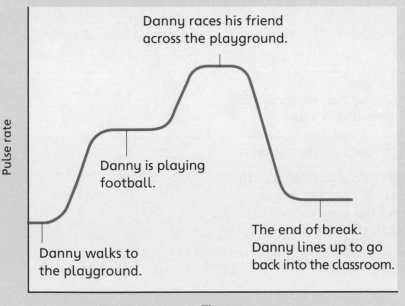

Danny races his friend across the playground.

Danny is playing football.

The end of break. Danny lines up to go back into the classroom.

Danny walks to the playground.

Pulse rate

Time

Test yourself!

1 What does blood carry around your body?

2 What pumps blood around your body?

3 Which kind of blood vessel takes blood to your muscles?

4 What is your pulse rate?

★5 Draw a table like this, and write down all the things you do during the day. Decide if your pulse rate would be low, medium or high for each activity.

Activity	Pulse rate
Eating breakfast	Low

Remember

Food, oxygen and other substances are carried around your body in your **blood**.

Your **heart pumps blood** around your body.

Blood **travels in tubes** called **blood vessels**.

Arteries take blood **away from your heart**, and **veins** take it back **to your heart**.

Your **pulse rate** is the **number of times your heart beats each minute**.

Your pulse rate goes **up when you run around**, and **goes down again when you rest**.

Health

When you are healthy you feel well, and you can work and play without getting too tired.

You need to look after your body if you want to stay healthy.

- You need to eat a **balanced diet** to make sure your body gets all the substances it needs. You can read more about balanced diets on pages 8 and 9.

Chicken with vegetables

Stir-fried vegetables with rice

Spaghetti and salad

- You need to exercise by running around, or by playing games like football or rounders. Exercise keeps your **heart** and **muscles** strong.
- If you are ill, you can often take a **drug** to help you to get better.

Sometimes you become ill because there are **micro-organisms** in the food that you eat. You can help to stop yourself getting stomach upsets by making sure that the food you eat has been cooked and stored properly. You can find out more about this on page 31.

What is a drug?

A **drug** is a substance that can change the way your body works. If you have a cough, a headache or a sore throat, you can buy **medicines**. Medicines are drugs that will help you to feel better. You can buy them in a chemist's shop or a supermarket. You must always take the correct amount of a medicine: if you do not take enough, it will not work properly, but if you take too much it can harm your body.

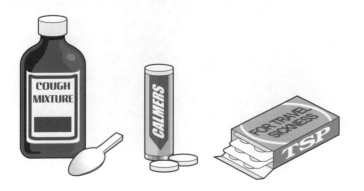

If you have a more serious illness, such as measles, or tonsillitis, you must see a doctor. The doctor will decide which medicines you need to make you better, and how much of the medicine you need to take.

Some medicines have **side effects**. A side effect is something that the medicine does to you that you did not want. For instance, if you take a medicine to stop you feeling sick on a long car journey, the medicine can often make you feel sleepy. Feeling sleepy is a side effect of the medicine. People take the medicine because they think it is better to feel sleepy than to feel sick!

Drugs that can be harmful

Some drugs are not medicines. For example, **alcohol** is a substance that is in beer, wine and some other drinks. People drink alcohol because it makes them feel good. However, if they drink too much they can feel very ill the next day, and too much alcohol can harm their body. If someone tries to drive a car when they have been drinking alcohol they may have an accident.

Tobacco contains a drug that people breathe in when they smoke cigarettes. Smoking tobacco makes some people feel good, but the substances in cigarette smoke can damage your heart and lungs.

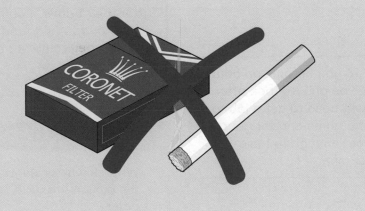

Test yourself!

1 Write down two things you need to do to stay healthy.

2 What are drugs?

3 a) What is a side effect?
  b) Give an example of a side effect.

4 Alcohol and tobacco are drugs. Why do people take these drugs?

5 Write down the different ways that alcohol and tobacco can harm your body.

★6 Explain how alcohol and tobacco could harm people who do not drink or smoke.

Remember

You need to **exercise** and to **eat a balanced diet** to stay healthy.

Drugs are substances that **change the way your body works**.

Some drugs are **medicines** that can make you better if you are ill.

Some drugs have **side effects**.

Alcohol and **tobacco** are drugs that can **harm** your body.

The human life cycle

You were very small when you were born, and your parents had to do everything for you – wash you, feed you, and change your nappies! Your body changes as you get older, and eventually you might have children of your own. All these changes are part of the human life cycle.

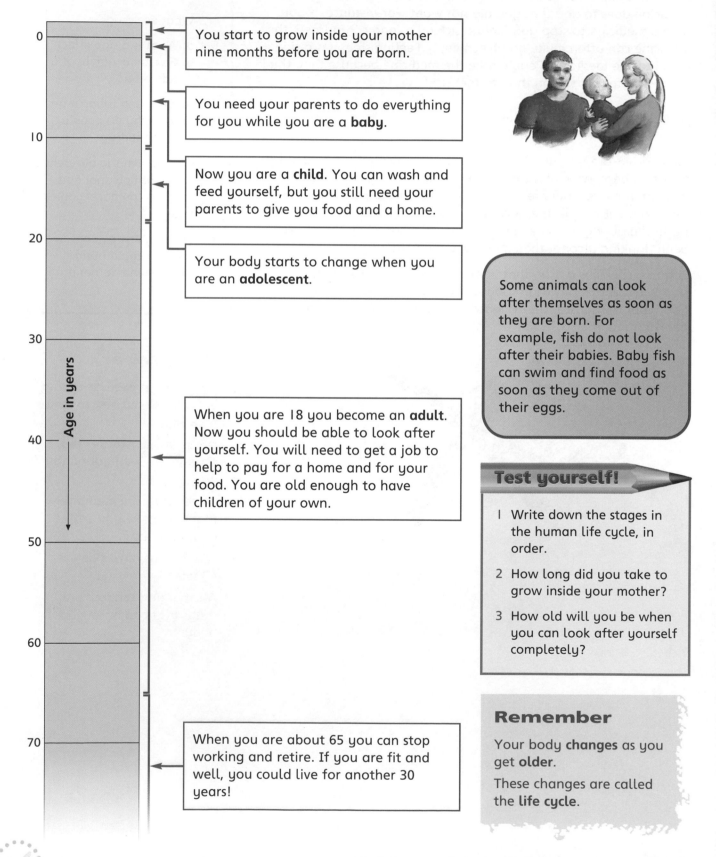

Age in years

You start to grow inside your mother nine months before you are born.

You need your parents to do everything for you while you are a **baby**.

Now you are a **child**. You can wash and feed yourself, but you still need your parents to give you food and a home.

Your body starts to change when you are an **adolescent**.

When you are 18 you become an **adult**. Now you should be able to look after yourself. You will need to get a job to help to pay for a home and for your food. You are old enough to have children of your own.

When you are about 65 you can stop working and retire. If you are fit and well, you could live for another 30 years!

Some animals can look after themselves as soon as they are born. For example, fish do not look after their babies. Baby fish can swim and find food as soon as they come out of their eggs.

Test yourself!

1 Write down the stages in the human life cycle, in order.

2 How long did you take to grow inside your mother?

3 How old will you be when you can look after yourself completely?

Remember

Your body **changes** as you get **older**.

These changes are called the **life cycle**.

Green plants

Plants are very important to us because they provide us with food. We eat some plants directly, like peas or apples. When we eat meat, we are eating an animal that has fed on plants.

Plants are living things. They have different parts, and all the parts need to work together to keep the plant healthy. Plants need light, air, water and warmth.

Parts of a plant

The **flowers** help the plant to reproduce. You will learn more about flowers and **reproduction** on pages 19 to 23.

Plants make food using their **leaves**. The leaves need light, air, water and warmth to make food.

The **stem** supports the plant. The stem has little tubes inside it. Water can travel up these tubes to reach the leaves.

The **roots** hold the plant in the **soil**, and take in water from the soil.

Test yourself!

1 Why do plants need leaves?

2 Why do plants need stems?

3 Why do plants need roots?

4 Look at these two plants.

a) Which plant will grow well?

b) Explain your answer (there are **two** reasons).

Remember

Plants need **light, air, water** and **warmth** to grow well.

Plants **make food** using their **leaves**.

Stems support the plant and **take water** up to the leaves.

Roots hold the plant in the **soil**, and **take in water**.

All the parts of a plant need to **work together**.

Plants and soil

Plants need light, air, water and warmth to grow well. Plants make new materials to help them grow using water, air and light. The new materials are made in the leaves. The process of making them is called photosynthesis.

Plants also need small amounts of other substances to keep them healthy. These nutrients dissolve in water in the soil and are taken in through the roots. If there are not enough nutrients in the soil to keep plants healthy, a farmer or a gardener might add fertiliser. The fertiliser adds nutrients to the soil. Plants that do not grow on farms or in gardens get their nutrients from animal droppings!

Different plants grow best in different soils, as you will see from the examples below.

Different plants, different needs

Marram grass grows on sand dunes, where there is not much water.

Bogbean plants grow in very wet places.

Different plants have different kinds of roots. This oak tree is very tall, and its roots go down a long way. The roots need to be very strong to support the tree in windy weather. All the little 'branches' in the roots help the tree to take in water.

This carrot plant does not need deep roots, because it is only a small plant and the wind cannot blow it over. The thick part of the root stores food.

Some bottles of fertiliser for house plants say 'plant food' on the label. This is not correct scientifically! Remember that plants make their own food in their leaves.

Test yourself!

1 What do plants need to make their own food?

2 Write down two things that plants take in through their roots.

3 Why do gardeners sometimes add fertiliser to the soil?

4 Why do tall trees need deeper roots than small plants?

★5 What kind of roots do you think grass plants have? Explain your answer.

Remember

Plants **make new materials** from **water**, **air** and **light**.

Plants **take in water** through their **roots**.

Plants also **take in nutrients**, which they need to keep **healthy**.

Different plants grow best in **different soils**.

Flowers

Plants **reproduce** (make new plants like themselves) by making **seeds**. The process of **reproduction** in plants is described in the diagram below. There are several stages in the **life cycle** of plants. You will find out more about the different stages on pages 21 to 23.

The new plant grows and forms **flowers**. Each flower has male and female organs. The male parts make **pollen**, and the female parts contain **ova** (eggs). (A single egg is called an **ovum**.)

A new plant starts to grow from the seed. This process is called **germination**.

Pollen from one flower is taken to another flower. This process is called **pollination**.

The seed falls off the plant. Most seeds **disperse** (they are taken away from the plant).

The fertilised ovum grows into a **seed**. Sometimes the seed is inside a **fruit**.

The pollen joins with an ovum in the flower. This is **fertilisation**.

Test yourself!

1 What happens during pollination?

2 What happens during fertilisation?

3 What does 'seed dispersal' mean?

4 What happens during germination?

Remember

Plants **reproduce** by making **seeds**.

There are **several stages** in the **life cycle** of a plant.

Parts of a flower

Plants need **flowers** to help them to reproduce. Each part of a flower has a job to do in the **reproduction** process.

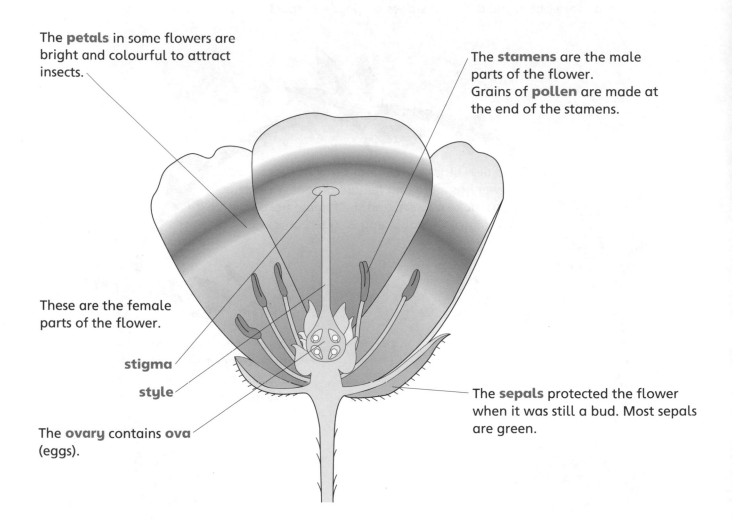

The **petals** in some flowers are bright and colourful to attract insects.

The **stamens** are the male parts of the flower. Grains of **pollen** are made at the end of the stamens.

These are the female parts of the flower.

stigma

style

The **ovary** contains **ova** (eggs).

The **sepals** protected the flower when it was still a bud. Most sepals are green.

Test yourself!

1 Which part of a flower makes pollen?

2 Which part of a flower contains the ova?

3 Why do flowers have petals?

4 What do the sepals do?

Remember

The **stamens** make **pollen**.

The **stigma**, **style** and **ovary** are the female parts.

Petals attract insects.

Pollination and fertilisation

Pollination

Pollen from flowers has to be carried to other flowers for plants to reproduce. This is pollination. It is an important part of the reproduction process. Pollen can be carried by insects or by the wind.

Some flowers make a sweet liquid called nectar that insects feed on. Pollen gets onto insects when they crawl inside the flower to get the nectar. The pollen is brushed off onto the stigma of the next flower the insects visit.

Flowers that are pollinated by insects usually have bright and colourful petals. These act like a signal to insects, to attract them to the nectar.

Did you know that grass has flowers? Grass pollen is carried from one plant to another by the wind, so the pollen grains are very small and light. The flowers do not need to attract insects, so they do not need to be large and colourful.

Fertilisation

When pollen lands on the stigma of a flower it starts to grow a little tube down the style. The pollen grain travels down this tube and joins an ovum. This is called fertilisation. When an ovum has been fertilised, it starts to grow into a seed. The ovary grows into a fruit.

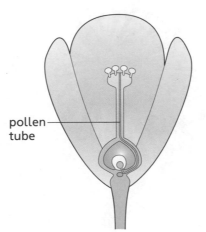

pollen tube

Test yourself!

1 Why do some flowers have brightly coloured petals?

2 Why do some flowers make nectar?

3 What does a fertilised ovum change into?

★4 Explain the difference between pollination and fertilisation.

Remember

Pollen can be transferred from one flower to another by insects or by the wind.

Pollen lands on the stigma, and grows a tube down the style.

Fertilisation happens when the pollen grain joins an ovum.

The fertilised ovum grows into a seed.

Seed dispersal

After **fertilisation**, a fertilised **ovum** will grow into a seed. When the **seeds** are ready, they fall off the plant and may start to grow into new plants.

If all the seeds landed around the parent plant they would be too crowded. They would not have enough space to grow, and they would not get enough light, air, water or nutrients. The seeds have to **disperse** (be spread out) so that they have room to grow.

The **wind** carries some seeds away from the parent plant. Seeds that are carried by the wind are light and fluffy, or have 'wings'.

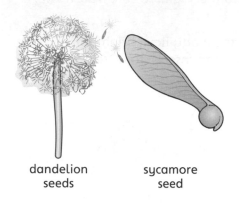

dandelion
seeds

sycamore
seed

Water disperses some seeds. For example, coconuts often land in the sea, and are carried away from the parent tree.

Some seeds are dispersed by **explosion**. Lupin seeds grow in pods. When the seeds are ready the pod splits open suddenly and the seeds are flung away.

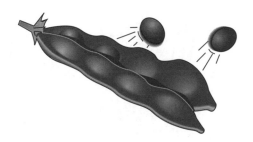

Animals disperse seeds. Apple seeds ('pips') are inside a juicy **fruit**. Animals eat the fruit, and the seeds inside pass right through their bodies and come out in their droppings.

Animals can also spread some seeds by carrying them around on their fur. Burdock seeds are covered in tiny hooks, which catch on fur.

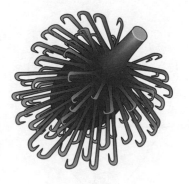

Test yourself!

1 Why do seeds need to be dispersed?

2 Write down four ways that seeds can be dispersed.

3 Why are dandelion seeds light and fluffy?

4 Why do some seeds have a juicy fruit around them?

Remember

Seeds need to be **dispersed** to get enough **space**, **light**, **air**, **water** and **nutrients** to **grow**.

Seeds can be **dispersed** by the **wind**, **water**, **animals** or by **explosion**.

Germination

Germination is when a seed starts to grow into a new plant. Seeds need water and warmth for germination, but they do not need light.

Jenny decided to investigate what seeds need to germinate. In order to do this she planned an experiment, which is described below.

Jenny's experiment

Jenny put some cress seeds into four different dishes and watered three of them. She left them in different places for a few days.

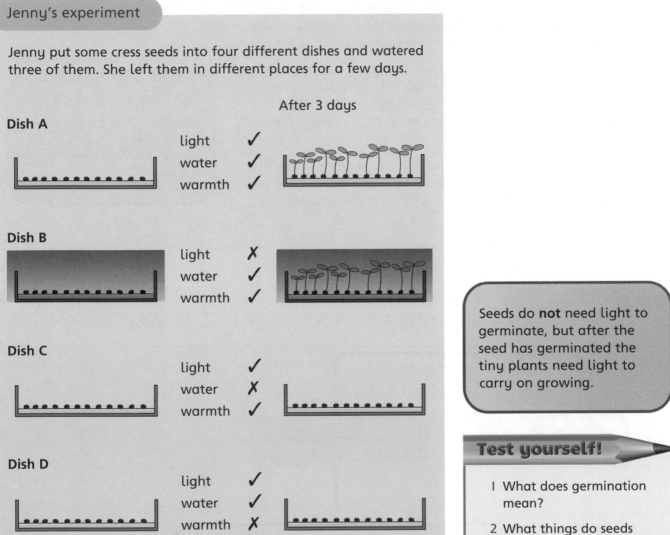

The seeds that Jenny put in Dishes A and B germinated. This shows that the seeds do not need light to germinate.

The seeds in Dish C did not germinate because they did not have any water.

The seeds in Dish D did not germinate because they were not warm enough.

Seeds do **not** need light to germinate, but after the seed has germinated the tiny plants need light to carry on growing.

Test yourself!

1 What does germination mean?

2 What things do seeds need to germinate?

★3 How can you show that seeds do not need light to germinate?

Remember

Germination is when seeds start to **grow** into **new plants**.

Seeds need **water** and **warmth** to **germinate**, but they **do not need light**.

Most seeds are spread in the autumn, when the weather is getting colder. If the seeds germinated straight away, the little plants would die over the winter. The seeds stay in the ground during the winter, and only germinate when the weather gets warmer again in the spring.

Sorting out living things

There are millions of different kinds of living things. It is very difficult to think about all these things separately, so scientists put them into groups. All the living things in a group are similar in some way.

The two main groups of living things are **animals** and **plants**. There are many differences between animals and plants, but the main difference is that plants can make their own food. Animals cannot do this – they have to eat plants or other animals for their food.

Animals are divided into smaller groups. One group contains all the animals that have backbones – this group includes humans. These animals are called **vertebrates**. The vertebrates are divided into five smaller groups, called amphibians, birds, fish, mammals and reptiles.

You can use a **key** to help you to work out which group something belongs to. Start at the top and answer each question. The red line on the key shows you how to work out which group **you** are in!

> You do not have to remember the names of all these groups, but you **do** need to know how to use keys!

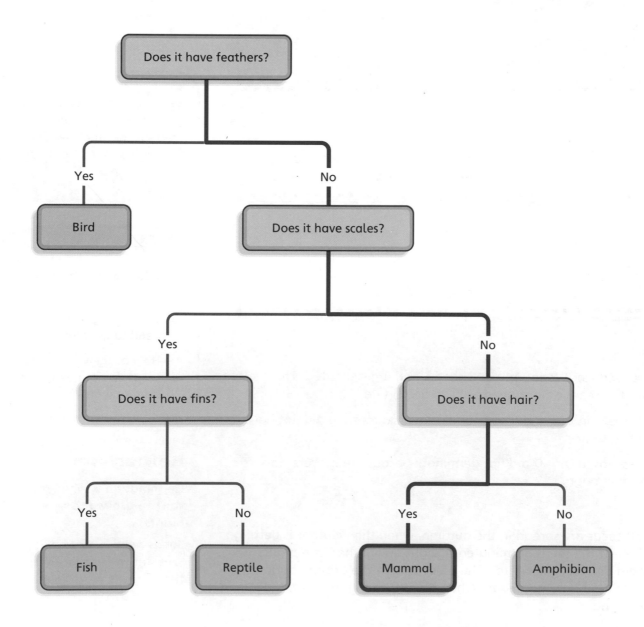

Looking at seabirds

Here is another key, similar to the one on page 24. This key helps you to identify some birds that live near the sea.

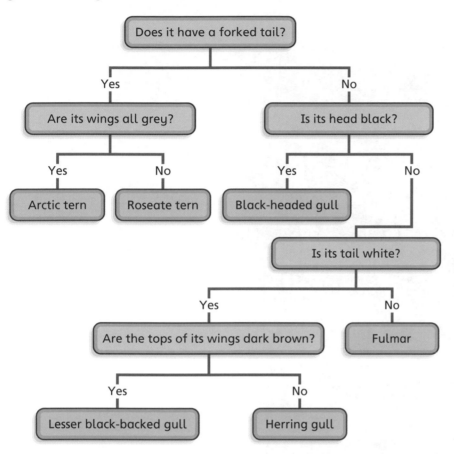

Does it have a forked tail?
- Yes → Are its wings all grey?
  - Yes → Arctic tern
  - No → Roseate tern
- No → Is its head black?
  - Yes → Black-headed gull
  - No → Is its tail white?
    - Yes → Are the tops of its wings dark brown?
      - Yes → Lesser black-backed gull
      - No → Herring gull
    - No → Fulmar

The example below shows you how the key can be used.

What is this bird?

You can use the key above to help you to identify this bird.

These are the answers to all the questions for this bird.

Does it have a forked tail?   *No.*

Is its head black?   *No.*

Is its tail white?   *Yes.*

Are the tops of its wings dark brown?   *No.*

Answer: It is a *herring gull*.

Remember

Scientists put living things into **groups** to make studying them easier.

The two main groups are **animals** and **plants**.

We can use **keys** to help us to **identify** living things.

Habitats

All living organisms live somewhere. The place where an organism lives is its **habitat**.

A woodland habitat

This is a woodland habitat. Rabbits, squirrels and birds live here. The woodland is also the habitat for insects, worms, grass, trees and bushes.

The habitat provides food for the organisms that live there. The rabbit eats grass, the squirrel eats acorns and other nuts, and the fox eats rabbits!

The animals and plants that live in the woodland are **adapted** to their habitat. This means that they have special features to help them to survive there.

The rabbit has large ears to listen for foxes, and strong hind legs to help it to run away.

Earthworms live in the **soil**. They have smooth, slippery skin to help them to slide through the soil. They eat dead **leaves**.

Different organisms need each other

The animals and plants in a habitat all need each other. Some animals need the plants for food. **Nutrients** in the plants get back into the soil in the animals' droppings, so the plants need the animals, too. Some plants need insects to pollinate them.

A pond habitat

This is a pond habitat. The conditions here are different to the conditions in a woodland, so different organisms live here. The fish and plants are all adapted to living underwater.

- The water lily has long stalks so that its **leaves** can reach the surface.
- The water boatman can walk on the surface of the water.
- The pike has large teeth to catch and eat other fish.

Some habitats can be quite small. A flower bed is a habitat. Even the little patch of soil underneath a stone can be a habitat, and may support hundreds of tiny creatures.

Test yourself!

1 What is a habitat?

2 a) Make a list of the organisms that live in a woodland habitat.
   b) Make a list of the organisms that live in a pond habitat.

3 a) What does 'adapted' mean?
   b) Describe two ways in which a rabbit is adapted to its habitat.
   c) Describe one way in which water lilies are adapted.

★4 Which organisms do you think you would find living in a habitat under a stone?

Remember

A **habitat** is the place where an **organism lives**.

The **plants** and **animals** in a habitat **need each other**.

Plants and animals are **adapted** to help them to live in **their habitat**.

Feeding

We all need to eat food to stay alive. Humans eat a mixture of plants and animals. Some animals only eat plants, and some animals only eat other animals.

Your beefburger is made from a cow.

Peas come from plants.

A plant is a **producer** because it produces food for animals to eat.

A human or any other animal is a **consumer**, because it consumes (eats) the food made by plants.

Food chains

A **food chain** shows the different animals that eat each other. The arrows show the direction that the food goes through the chain. Food chains always start with a plant, because plants make their own food using light, water and air.

An animal that only eats plants is a **herbivore**. In the food chain shown below, the tadpoles are herbivores.

An animal that only eats other animals is a **carnivore**. The perch and pike are carnivores.

An **omnivore** eats plants **and** other animals.

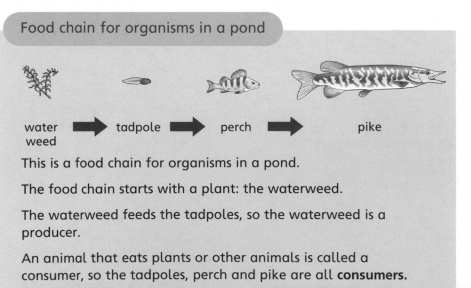

Food chain for organisms in a pond

water weed ➡ tadpole ➡ perch ➡ pike

This is a food chain for organisms in a pond.

The food chain starts with a plant: the waterweed.

The waterweed feeds the tadpoles, so the waterweed is a producer.

An animal that eats plants or other animals is called a consumer, so the tadpoles, perch and pike are all **consumers**.

A **predator** eats other animals. The pike and perch are **predators** because they eat other animals.

Prey are animals that are eaten by other animals. The perch and tadpoles are **prey**, because other animals eat them.

Vegetarians and vegans

Humans are omnivores because they can eat plants and meat. However, some people choose to be herbivores: these people are known as vegetarians. Most vegetarians eat eggs and cheese and drink milk as well as eating foods from plants.

Some people are vegans, which means that they do not eat anything that comes from animals. Vegans have to be very careful to eat a balanced diet. Look back at pages 8 and 9, and think about how you could get a balanced diet if you could not eat anything that came from animals.

Test yourself!

Look at this food chain to help you to answer the questions.

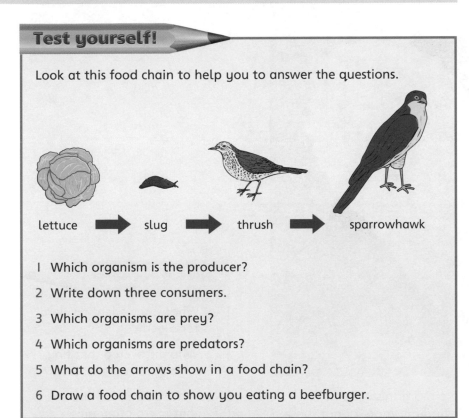

lettuce ➡ slug ➡ thrush ➡ sparrowhawk

1 Which organism is the producer?

2 Write down three consumers.

3 Which organisms are prey?

4 Which organisms are predators?

5 What do the arrows show in a food chain?

6 Draw a food chain to show you eating a beefburger.

Remember

We all need to eat **food** to live.

Plants are **producers**, and **animals** are **consumers**.

Predators eat **prey**.

A **food chain** shows **which animals eat each other**.

Food chains always **start** with a **plant**.

An animal can be both a predator and prey. For instance, in the food chain for organisms in a pond (page 28) the perch eats tadpoles, so it is a predator. Pike eat the perch, so the perch is also prey for a different animal.

What makes you ill?

Do you remember being ill? You have probably had a cold and an upset stomach at some time. You might even have had an illness like measles or chicken pox.

Some people used to think that smelly air caused diseases. Others believed that the stars affected people and sometimes made them ill. In 1865, a French scientist called Louis Pasteur did an experiment and showed that tiny organisms cause diseases.

Micro-organisms that cause disease

The tiny organisms that Louis Pasteur discovered are called **micro-organisms**, or **microbes**. In everyday life we usually call them **germs**. Micro-organisms are very small. You can only see them when you use a microscope.

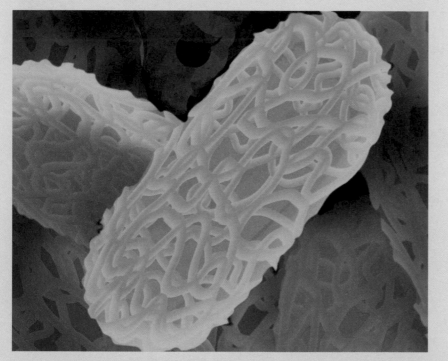

There are lots of different kinds of micro-organism. Some micro-organisms are useful. You will find out more about these on pages 32 and 33. Other micro-organisms cause diseases like colds, flu, chicken pox and food poisoning. Microbes in your mouth feed on bits of food stuck between your teeth, and cause tooth decay or gum disease.

Other causes of disease

Not all diseases are caused by micro-organisms. For instance, scurvy is a disease that can be caused by not having enough Vitamin C. Heart disease can be caused by eating too many fatty foods. A healthy diet helps you to avoid many kinds of disease. You can find out more about healthy diets on page 8.

Test yourself!

1 What is the scientific word for a germ?

2 Who discovered that tiny organisms cause diseases?

3 Write down four diseases that micro-organisms cause.

4 Write down two diseases that are not caused by micro-organisms.

Remember

Micro-organisms (or **microbes**) are very tiny **organisms**.

Some micro-organisms can cause **diseases**.

Keeping healthy

Many diseases are caused by **micro-organisms**. You can protect yourself against some of these diseases.

Preventing tooth decay

Tooth **decay** is caused by micro-organisms feeding on bits of food left in your mouth. You can keep your teeth and gums healthy by brushing your teeth twice a day, and not eating sweets between meals.

Coughs and sneezes spread diseases ...

Some micro-organisms cause colds or flu. When a person with a cold sneezes or coughs, the micro-organisms spread through the air and other people can catch the disease. You should always sneeze into a handkerchief and put your hand over your mouth when you cough. Doctors and dentists often wear face masks, so they do not breathe any micro-organisms onto their patients.

How to prevent food poisoning

Food poisoning (an 'upset stomach') is caused by micro-organisms in your food. The micro-organisms grow on the food, and can make you very ill if you eat them. They do not grow very fast when they are cold, and they are killed when you cook the food. Keep food safe by following the six simple rules that are shown below.

Six rules for safe food

+ Wash your hands before touching food

+ Keep food in a fridge

+ Check the 'use by' date on the packet, and never eat food that has passed it

+ Make sure that meat or fish has been cooked before you eat it

+ Keep raw meat or fish away from cooked food

+ Use different knives and different chopping boards for raw meat and cooked meat

Test yourself!

1 How can you prevent tooth decay?

2 How can you stop colds spreading?

3 Write down three rules for keeping food safe.

★4 Why do you think you should keep raw meat away from cooked food?

Remember

Micro-organisms can cause diseases.

Prevent tooth decay by **cleaning your teeth twice a day**.

Stop colds spreading by always **sneezing into a handkerchief**.

Prevent food poisoning by following the **six simple rules**.

Decay

Have you ever seen a mouldy apple? It is brown and soggy, because micro-organisms called **moulds** have grown on it and make it decay. You can keep food for longer before it decays if you put it in a fridge, because moulds do not grow very fast when it is cold.

This apple is fresh.

This apple is decaying.

Uses of decay

Decay is not useful when it makes food go 'off', but it is very useful in nature. Some examples are described below.

It stops rubbish piling up

Dead animals and insects decay, and so do dead leaves and dead trees. Some rubbish also decays, such as vegetable peelings, old wood, and other things made from plants. Imagine what would happen if rubbish and dead material did not decay! Decay stops rubbish piling up for ever.

It recycles nutrients

Decay is also useful because it recycles nutrients. Nutrients are substances that plants need to help them to grow. Plants get their nutrients from the soil, and the nutrients end up in leaves and other parts of the plants. When leaves fall off trees and decay, the nutrients return to the soil so they can be used again. If dead leaves did not decay, the soil would soon run out of nutrients.

Some materials do not decay. Micro-organisms cannot feed on plastics and metals, so these materials do not decay when we throw them away.

Test yourself!

1   What makes decay happen?

2   Write down an example of when decay is not useful.

3   Explain one way in which decay is useful.

Remember

Decay happens when **micro-organisms feed on material**.

Decay **recycles nutrients**, so they can be used again.

Some materials, like **plastic** and **metal, do not decay**.

Using micro-organisms to make food

Some **micro-organisms** are very useful in making food. All the foods shown here are made using micro-organisms.

beer
bread
yoghurt
wine
Marmite   cheese   Quorn

For example, yoghurt is made from milk. A special type of micro-organism is added to the milk, and as it feeds on the milk it produces other substances that turn the milk into yoghurt.

How yeast can be used to make bread

Yeast is a micro-organism that is used to make some kinds of bread. The bread dough needs to be kept warm to help the yeast to grow. As the yeast grows, it feeds on sugar in the bread dough and makes a **gas** – this is shown in Leela's experiment, which is described below. The gas makes the dough rise, and when the bread is cooked you can see lots of tiny holes in the bread formed by bubbles of gas.

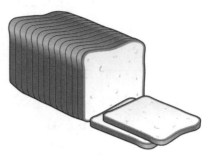

Leela's experiment

Leela did an experiment to find out what yeast needs to help it to grow. She set up four test tubes like this:

Leave in a warm place.   Leave in a cool place.

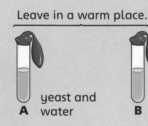

A yeast and water   **B** yeast and sugar and water   **C** yeast and water   **D** yeast and sugar and water

After a few hours, Leela found that the test tubes looked like this:

  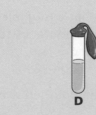

A   **B**   **C**   **D**

The balloon on test tube B is full of gas made by the yeast. The yeast has only grown in test tube B, which contained yeast and sugar and water, and had been left in a warm place. This was the only test tube that provided the yeast with both food (sugar) and warmth. Leela's experiment shows that yeast needs food and warmth to help it grow.

Test yourself!

1 Write down four different foods that are made using micro-organisms.

2 How does yeast help bread to rise?

3 What does yeast need to help it to grow?

★4 How do you know that yeast is a living organism?

Remember

Micro-organisms can be used to **make some foods**.

Micro-organisms are **living things** that need **food** and **warmth** to **grow**.

Materials and their uses

Look around you and you will see things made of lots of different materials. Windows are made of glass. Doors and floors are made from wood, and door handles are made from metal. Glass is used for windows because it is **transparent** (see through), and wood is used for floors because it is strong.

When we describe what a material is like we are describing its properties. We use different materials for different jobs, because they have different properties. The words below all describe different properties.

Words used to describe the properties of materials

There are many words that can be used to describe the properties of materials. Here are some examples of just a few.

Property	Meaning
absorbent	soaks up water easily
brittle	breaks easily if you hit it
cheap	costs less money to buy it
flexible	bendy
hard	difficult to dent
light	easy to lift, not too heavy to carry
strong	difficult to break
transparent	see through

Some materials have properties that need more than one word to describe them. For example, when you are choosing a material you might need to consider:

- whether **heat travels through the material easily** (heat does not travel through wood so this is a good material to use for the handles of things that get hot. You can find out more about this on page 38.)

- whether electricity **travels through the material easily** (electricity does not travel through plastic so this is a good material to use for the handset of a telephone, which you need to hold. You can find out more about this on page 39.)

- whether the material **looks nice** (for example, polished wood is shiny and can have attractive patterns in it).

Most materials have more than one property. A material is used for a particular job because of one or two of its properties.

Windows are made from glass because it is **transparent** and **hard**. Glass is also **brittle**, which is not a useful property!

Towels are made from cotton because it is **absorbent** and **flexible**.

Tables and cupboards are made from wood because it is **hard** and **strong**. It is also easy to make wood into different shapes, and to paint or polish it so that it looks nice.

Saucepans are made of a metal called aluminium. Aluminium is **light**, so the pans are easy to lift.

Knives and spoons are made from steel, which is a strong and cheap metal.

Cooking spoons are made of wood, because heat does not travel through wood easily.

Drinks bottles are make of plastic, because it is **light** and not **brittle**. It is also easy to make it into the right shape.

Plugs are made from plastic, because electricity does not go through plastic. This stops you getting an electric shock!

Mugs and plates are made from ceramic materials, because they are **hard** and heat does not travel through them easily. Ceramics are also **brittle**, which is not a useful property.

Test yourself!

1. a) Glass is used to make windows. Write down two **useful** properties of glass.
   b) Write down one property of glass that is **not** useful.

2. Why are towels made from cotton?

3. Why is some furniture made of wood?

4. Why are plugs made from plastic?

★5. Jumpers are often made from wool. What are the useful properties of wool?

Remember

Different materials have **different properties**, such as being strong, flexible or transparent.

We **choose materials** to make things because of their **useful properties**.

Testing materials

Scientists need to be able to test different materials to find out which one is best for the job. Scientists must make sure that each test they make is a **fair test**. You can find out more about fair tests on page 82.

Kitchen towels are made of paper. They are used to mop up spills. Samir tested different kinds of paper to find out which kind is best for kitchen towels.

Samir's experiment

Samir tested paper from a newspaper and from an exercise book, and he tested a piece of kitchen towel.

He cut all the paper into the same size squares.

Samir poured a small amount of water onto the table, and then mopped it up using the squares of newspaper. He counted how many squares of paper he needed to mop up all the water. He did the same thing again with the exercise book paper and the kitchen towel. He used the same amount of water each time. The table shows his results.

Paper	Number of pieces needed
newspaper	2
exercise book paper	4
kitchen towel	I

Samir found that the best paper for mopping up spills is the kitchen towel, because it did not take many pieces of paper to soak up all the water.

Samir's test was fair, because he cut all the paper into the same size squares, and he used the same amount of water each time.

Test yourself!

I Write down two things that Samir did to make his test fair.

Remember

You can **test materials** to find which one is **best for a job**.

Hot and cold

Temperature is a way of saying how hot or cold something is. You can measure the temperature of something using a **thermometer**. The units for temperature are **degrees Celsius** (°C).

This thermometer is measuring the temperature of the air in the room. It is 21°C.

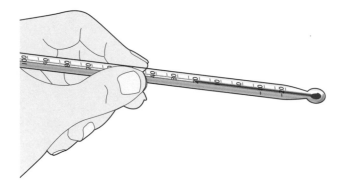

The water in this bowl is at a temperature of 0°C. It is colder than the air, so heat from the air around it will warm it up until it is the same temperature as the air in the room.

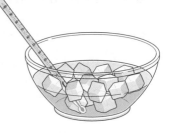

The temperature of this water is 60°C. Heat from the water will spread into the air around it, and the water will cool down until it is the same temperature as the air in the room.

You can measure the temperature of water as it cools down and you can show the results in a graph.

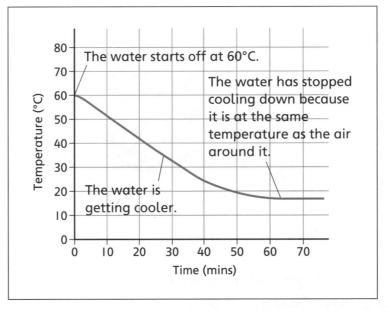

The water starts off at 60°C.

The water has stopped cooling down because it is at the same temperature as the air around it.

The water is getting cooler.

Test yourself!

1 What are the units for measuring temperature?

2 What do you use to measure temperature?

3 The temperature in your bedroom is 23°C. If you leave a cup of tea in your room, what temperature will it be the next morning?

Remember

You **measure temperature** using a **thermometer**.

The **units for temperature** are **degrees Celsius** (°C).

Hot things will **cool down** until they are the **same temperature** as the **air around them**.

Cool things will **warm up** until they are the **same temperature** as the **air around them**.

Conducting heat

Heat can travel through some materials better than others.

Thermal conductors

Heat can travel through metals very easily. This is why you can burn your fingers if you pick up a teaspoon that has been standing in hot tea for a few minutes. Metal is a good **thermal** conductor.

Thermal insulators

Heat does not travel very well through wood. Wood is a **thermal insulator**. Plastic is also a thermal insulator. Cooking spoons are usually made from wood or plastic, so that the heat from cooking food does not travel up them and burn your hand.

Keeping things warm

Thermal insulators are very useful for keeping you warm. Jumpers keep you warm because they have lots of little pockets of trapped air. Trapped air is a good thermal insulator.

This mug is made of plastic and foam, which are good thermal insulators. The hot coffee inside it will stay hot for a long time, because heat cannot get out very easily.

Keeping things cool

Thermal insulators can also keep cold things cold.

This cool box is made of plastic and foam, which are good thermal insulators. It is used to keep food cold. Heat from the air outside cannot get into the box, so the food stays cold.

Test yourself!

1 Write down one material that is a good thermal conductor.

2 Write down two materials that are good thermal insulators.

★3 Duvets are filled with feathers. Explain why duvets keep you warm.

Remember

Thermal conductors let heat travel through them easily.

Metals are good thermal conductors.

Thermal insulators do not let heat travel through them.

Wood and plastic are good thermal insulators.

Conducting electricity

Some materials let electricity flow through them. A material that lets electricity flow through it is called an **electrical** conductor. A material that does not let electricity flow through it is called an **electrical** insulator.

Is it a conductor or an insulator?

You can test a material to see if it is a conductor or an insulator using a circuit like this.

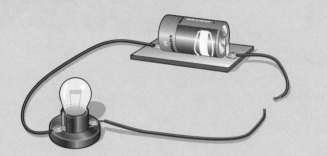

Put the material you are testing in the gap and join it to the wires on each side. If the material is an electrical conductor, electricity will flow through it and the bulb will light. You can find out more about circuits on page 61.

Metals are good electrical conductors. Materials that are good electrical conductors are usually good thermal conductors as well.

Plastic, rubber and wood are all good electrical insulators.

You can find out more about circuits on page 61.

Test yourself!

1 Write down one material that is an electrical insulator.

2 Why are the pins in a plug made from metal?

3 Why are wires covered in plastic?

Remember

Electrical conductors let electricity flow through them easily.

Metals are good electrical conductors.

Electrical insulators do not let electricity flow through them.

Plastics are good **electrical insulators**.

Using conductors and insulators in a plug

Different parts of a plug are made from metal (an electrical **conductor**) and plastic (an electrical **insulator**), because each part of the plug has a different job.

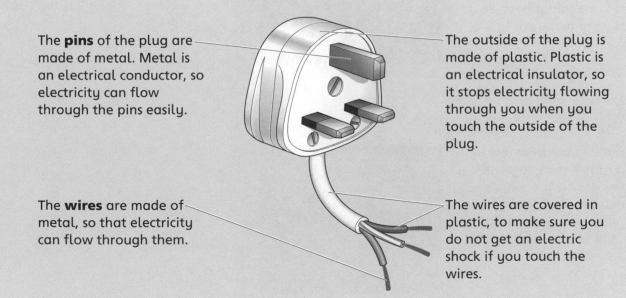

The **pins** of the plug are made of metal. Metal is an electrical conductor, so electricity can flow through the pins easily.

The outside of the plug is made of plastic. Plastic is an electrical insulator, so it stops electricity flowing through you when you touch the outside of the plug.

The **wires** are made of metal, so that electricity can flow through them.

The wires are covered in plastic, to make sure you do not get an electric shock if you touch the wires.

Rocks

Houses and walls can be made of bricks, concrete or rock. Bricks and concrete are made from other materials, but **rocks** can be dug out of the ground in **quarries**. Small pieces of rock are called **stones**, and very small pieces are sometimes called **pebbles**. Rocks are always underneath us, but we cannot always see them.

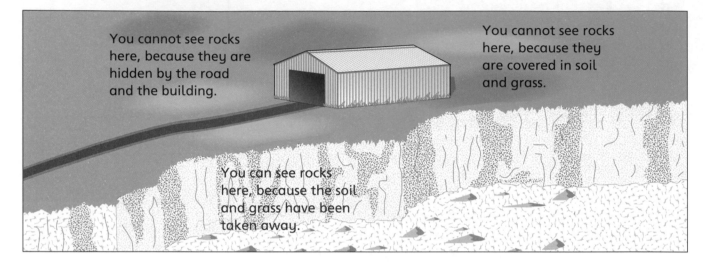

You cannot see rocks here, because they are hidden by the road and the building.

You cannot see rocks here, because they are covered in soil and grass.

You can see rocks here, because the soil and grass have been taken away.

Some different types of rock

There are lots of different kinds of rock. Some rocks are hard and some are soft. Some rocks are **permeable**, which means that water can run through them. Rocks are made of different **grains** stuck together.

Granite

Granite is a hard rock. It is made from different coloured grains. The grains have sharp edges, and some of them are quite big. Granite is often used for steps to buildings because it does not wear away easily.

Sandstone

Sandstone is made from lots of rounded grains stuck together. The grains are all the same size. It is sometimes used for building walls, but it is not as hard as granite and can be worn away by the weather.

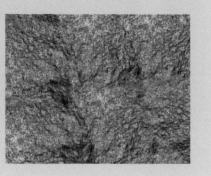

Chalk

Chalk is a soft, white rock, with very small grains. Chalk can be used for drawing, because the grains rub off very easily.

Marble

Marble is a hard rock with very tiny grains. Marble is used for making statues, because it lasts a long time and is nice to look at.

When you describe the size and shape of the grains in a rock, you are describing the **texture** of the rock.

Test yourself!

1 Write down two reasons why you might not be able to see rocks underneath you.

2 Write down the names of two building materials that are not rocks.

3 Why is marble often used for statues?

4 a) What does 'permeable' mean?
   b) How can you find out if a rock is permeable?

★5 Which kind of rock would be best for the wall of a building? Explain your answer.

Testing rocks

Sometimes you might want to find out about the **properties** of a rock. Two tests for rocks are described below.

Which rock is the hardest?

You can find out which rocks are the hardest by rubbing different rocks together. The harder rock will rub pieces off the softer rock. For example, if you rub a piece of granite against a piece of sandstone, bits of sandstone will be rubbed off because granite is harder than sandstone.

Is this rock permeable?

You can find out if a rock is permeable by dropping water on it. Look at the water carefully, and see if it soaks into the rock. If it soaks in quickly, the rock is permeable.

Remember

Rocks are **underneath us** everywhere, even though we cannot always see them.

Rocks are made from **grains stuck together**.

Rocks can be **hard or soft**, and **some rocks are permeable**.

Soils

Soil is made from bits of rock and from decayed bits of dead plants and animals. The decaying materials provide nutrients for plants growing in the soil. You can find out more about decay and nutrients on page 32, and about soil and air on page 45.

Soil can have different layers in it.

The top layer has lots of dead plant material in it. It is usually dark brown.

The next layer does not have much dead plant material. It is usually light brown.

The layer of soil next to the rock has lots of stones in it.

Rock.

There are different soils in different parts of Britain, depending on the kinds of rock they are made from. Some examples are described below.

Sandy soils

Sandy soils are crumbly. Water runs quickly through sandy soils, because there are lots of air spaces.

Chalky soils

Like sandy soils, chalky soils are crumbly. Water runs quickly through chalky soil.

Clay soils

Clay soils are sticky and muddy when they are wet. Clay soils hold a lot of water, but when they dry out they go very hard and crack.

Loam soils

Loam soils have a mixture of sand and clay particles. They are the best soils for growing plants.

Test yourself!

1 Where do the nutrients in soil come from?

2 Name one kind of soil that holds a lot of water.

3 Name one kind of soil that has a lot of air spaces in it.

Remember

Soil is made from **bits of rock** and **decayed animals and plants**.

Soil can have **different layers** in it.

The **kind of soil** depends on the **kind of rock under the soil**.

Solids and liquids

On pages 34 and 35, you learned how to describe the **properties** of different materials. Another way of describing the properties of a material is to say if it is **solid** or **liquid**. Solids and liquids have different properties.

The properties of solids

Solids are usually hard, and do not change shape. They are very difficult to squash, and their volume (the amount of space they take up) does not change. Wood and metal are solids.

The properties of liquids

Liquids are runny. The shape of a liquid depends on the shape of the container you put it into. Liquids do not change volume, even though they can change shape. It is very difficult to squash liquids. Water and honey are liquids.

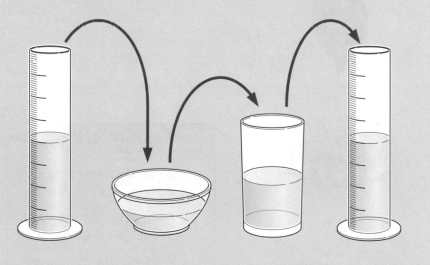

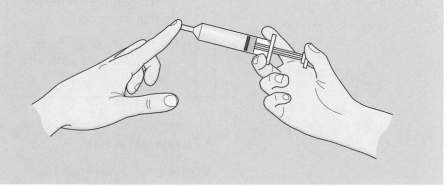

Test yourself!

1 Write down the names of two solid materials.

2 Write down the names of two liquid materials.

3 Write down the names of two solid materials that sometimes behave like liquids.

Remember

Solids are **hard**, and **keep the same shape**.

Liquids are **runny**, and **do not keep the same shape**. They take up the **shape of the container** they are in.

Solids and liquids always keep the **same volume**.

Solids that are **made of very tiny particles** can **behave like liquids** in some ways.

It is difficult to decide whether some things are solids or liquids! You can pour sand like a liquid, but each separate particle of sand is a solid. You can also pour rice, flour and salt. These materials are all solids, but they behave like liquids in some ways because they are made of very tiny pieces.

Gases

Air is not a **solid** or a **liquid**. The air is made of gases. You cannot see air, but you know it is real because you can often feel it, especially when it is moving.

Different types of gases

There are lots of different types of **gas**:

- Part of the air is made of **oxygen** gas. All living things need oxygen to stay alive.
- The bubbles in fizzy drinks are **carbon dioxide**.
- Some balloons are filled with **helium** gas, which makes them float.
- The gas that burns in cookers is called **natural gas**.

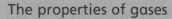
The properties of gases

Gases have different **properties** to solids and liquids.

You can squash a gas quite easily, but you cannot squash solids and liquids.

Gases spread out to fill the container they are in. You can smell perfume all over a room, because the perfume evaporates into a gas and the gas spreads out.

Test yourself!

1 Write down one reason we know that air is real.

2 Write down the names of four different gases.

3 Write down two ways in which gases are different to liquids.

★4 Write down one way in which gases are similar to liquids.

Remember

Gases can be **squashed**, and **spread out to fill their container**.

There are lots of **different gases**, which have **different uses**.

Investigating gases

It is difficult to investigate a **gas** because you cannot see it. You need to look for other evidence to show that gases are real.

Air fills gaps

A sponge has lots of gaps in it. You can show that the gaps are full of air by squeezing the sponge under water. You will see lots of bubbles, which are made by the air that you have squeezed out of the sponge.

Soil is made of lots of small particles. Between the particles there are gaps, which are full of air. If you pour water onto soil you will see bubbles of air coming up, because the water pushes the air out of the gaps between the particles.

Air has weight

You can show that air is real because it has **weight**. A balloon full of air weighs more than an empty balloon.

Ben's experiment

Ben did an experiment to find out how much air is in different soils.

sandy soil
clay soil

Ben poured water onto the soil a little bit at a time, until no more water would soak in. He looked at how much water was left in the measuring cylinders.

sandy soil
clay soil

The sandy soil soaked up the most water. The water went into the spaces that were full of air, so the sandy soil had the most air in it to start with.

Test yourself!

1 Describe how you can show that the gaps in a sponge are full of air.

2 How do you know that soil has air in it?

3 Write down two things that Ben did to make his test a **fair test**. (You can find out more about fair tests on page 82.)

Remember

You can tell that air is real because it **has weight**.

The **gaps** in sponges and in soil are **full of air**.

Changing state

Water can be a **solid** (ice), a **liquid** (water) or a **gas** (**water vapour**, or steam). Solids, liquids and gases are the three **states of matter**.

The **state** of matter can change. If you let ice warm up, it will **melt** and form a liquid. If you cool the water down to 0°C it will **freeze** and turn back into ice.

Liquids can evaporate. Water in puddles dries up because the water **evaporates**. **Evaporation** turns water into a gas called **water vapour**. If you cool the water vapour down again, it will **condense** and turn back into liquid water. This liquid water is called **condensation**.

The 'cloud' that you can see above a kettle when it is boiling is not steam. It is tiny drops of liquid water.

What happens when you boil water?

If you heat water up to 100°C it starts **boiling**. The water is evaporating so fast that bubbles of water vapour are formed in the water.

The water vapour cools down when it leaves the kettle. It condenses and forms tiny drops of water.

Water vapour (or steam) fills the kettle. It is invisible.

Bubbles of water vapour are forming in the liquid.

Water at 100°C.

Test yourself!

1 What are the three states of matter?

2 How can you turn liquid water into ice?

3 What does condensation mean?

★4 What is the difference between evaporation and boiling?

Remember

The **three states** of matter are **solids**, **liquids** and **gases**.

The names for **changes of state** are **melting**, **evaporating**, **condensing** and **freezing**.

Changes of state are **reversible** changes.

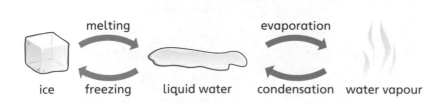

melting   evaporation

ice   freezing   liquid water   condensation   water vapour

A change of state is a **reversible change**, because you can change a substance back to its original state by changing the **temperature**.

Evaporation

Evaporation is what happens when a **liquid** turns into a **gas**.

When you wash clothes, they feel wet because there is a lot of liquid water in the cloth. When you hang the clothes up to dry, the water evaporates. It turns into a gas (**water vapour**) and mixes with the air.

Speeding up evaporation

Imagine that you have a big pile of wet washing, which you have just taken out of the washing machine. You can speed up evaporation in three ways.

1   **Spread out the washing** so that there is a bigger area for the water to evaporate from.

2   **Dry the clothes where it is warm**. Water evaporates faster when it is warm.

3   **Dry the clothes in a breeze**. The moving air carries the evaporated water away so that more water can evaporate into the air.

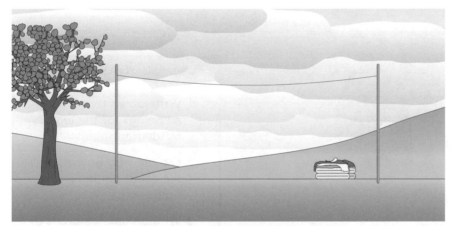

This washing will take a long time to dry.

This washing will dry quickly.

You can also dry clothes in a tumble dryer, if you have one. A tumble dryer blows warm air through the clothes. The warmth helps water to evaporate, and the moving air carries the water vapour away.

Test yourself!

1   What does evaporation mean?

2   Describe three ways of speeding up evaporation, and explain why they work.

Remember

When a liquid **evaporates**, it turns into a **gas**.

Evaporation happens **faster** if the water is **warm**, if there is a **large area**, and if the **evaporated water** is **blown away**.

Condensation

When **water vapour** cools down it **condenses** and turns into a **liquid**.
You can often see **condensation** happening in the bathroom.

Condensation in the bathroom

Imagine that you have just had a hot bath or shower and you are
standing at the sink, washing your face. Some of the hot water
has evaporated. This **evaporation** means that there is a lot of
water vapour in the air. The water vapour cools down when it hits
the mirror, and condenses to form little drops of water. These
drops of water are also called condensation. You know that they
are there when you can't see your face in the mirror!

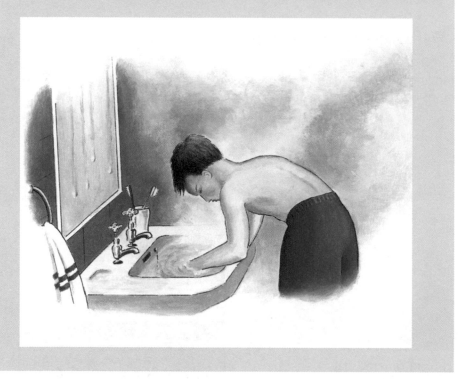

The word condensation has two meanings – it means water
vapour changing into liquid water, and it also means the tiny
drops of water that form on windows or other cold surfaces.

There is water vapour in the air all the time. If you take a can of
drink out of the fridge you will see some condensation on the
outside. Water vapour in the air cools down when it touches the
cold can, and it condenses to form drops of water.

There is a lot of water vapour in the air that you breathe out. The
air you breathe out is warm, because it has been inside your body.
When you breathe it out on a cold day the water vapour cools
down and condenses.

Test yourself!

1 Write down two
meanings for the word
condensation.

2 Explain why you often
see condensation in the
bathroom.

3 Why do you see drops of
water on the outside of a
can of cold drink?

★4 Why can you only see
your breath on a cold
day?

Remember

Gases change to liquids
by **condensation**.

Condensation happens
when **water vapour cools
down**.

The **drops of water**
formed by condensation are
also called **condensation**.

Melting and boiling

Materials change **state** when they are heated up or cooled down. If you heat ice, it will **melt** when it reaches 0°C. If you cool down **liquid** water, it will **freeze** when it reaches 0°C. This is the **freezing temperature** of water.

Liquid water can evaporate to form a **gas**. This can happen at any **temperature**, but if you heat the water to 100°C, **evaporation** will happen as fast as it can. Bubbles of gas form inside the liquid, and we say that the liquid is **boiling**. The **boiling temperature** of water is 100°C.

Watching what happens when ice is heated

The graph below shows what happens to the temperature of ice as it is heated up.

Remember

Ice melts at 0°C and **water boils at 100°C**.

The temperature of **liquid water** never goes above **100°C**.

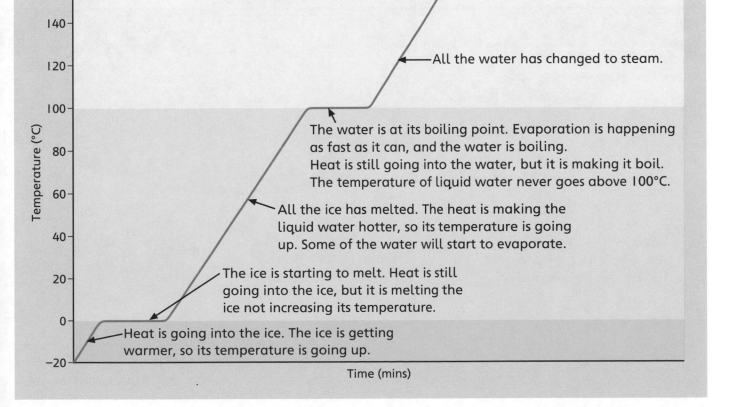

All the water has changed to steam.

The water is at its boiling point. Evaporation is happening as fast as it can, and the water is boiling.
Heat is still going into the water, but it is making it boil.
The temperature of liquid water never goes above 100°C.

All the ice has melted. The heat is making the liquid water hotter, so its temperature is going up. Some of the water will start to evaporate.

The ice is starting to melt. Heat is still going into the ice, but it is melting the ice not increasing its temperature.

Heat is going into the ice. The ice is getting warmer, so its temperature is going up.

Time (mins)

Temperature (°C)

The water cycle

The water that comes out of your taps was once in the sea. The **evaporation** of water from the sea, lakes and rivers forms water vapour. The **water vapour** condenses to form clouds, and then the water falls as rain. Our drinking water comes from rain that is trapped in reservoirs or flows into rivers. The water has to be cleaned before we can use it. When we have used the water it is put into drains, and eventually gets back to the sea.

These changes form the water cycle.

Water vapour in the air cools down and condenses. We see the condensed water as clouds.

Water in the clouds can fall as rain.

Plants take in water from the soil. Some of this water evaporates from the plants.

Some water evaporates from lakes and rivers.

Water evaporates from the sea. Evaporation happens fastest in warm places.

Water in rivers and lakes runs into the sea.

Water from toilets, sinks and baths runs into the drains. This water is treated at sewage works to make it safe, then it is put back into rivers or the sea.

If the air is very cold, the water in the clouds can freeze to form hail or snow.

Snow will melt when the Sun warms it up.

Some water is trapped in reservoirs.

Water from rain or melted snow runs into rivers and lakes.

Water from rivers, lakes, reservoirs or wells is cleaned before it is sent to houses.

Some water soaks into the ground. We can get this water by digging wells.

Test yourself!

1 Where can water evaporate from in the water cycle?

2 How do clouds form?

3 What happens to rain when it falls on the land?

4 What happens to water before it comes out of our taps?

5 What happens to water after we have used it?

★6 Water can go through these changes of state on its way around the water cycle:

liquid → gas → liquid → solid → liquid

Explain where in the water cycle each of these changes could happen.

Remember

Water **evaporates from the sea** and then **condenses to form clouds**.

Water **falls from clouds as rain**, and **runs into rivers and lakes**.

Water has to be **cleaned** before we use it.

Used water is **treated in sewage works** before it is put back into the sea.

Mixtures and filtering

Lots of different things jumbled up together are a **mixture**. For example, if you put peas and sand together you have a mixture.

Using a sieve

You can separate a mixture using a **sieve**. A sieve has lots of small holes in it. Think again about the mixture of sand and peas. The sand grains are small enough to go through the holes, so they fall out of the sieve. The peas are too big to fit through the holes, so they are trapped in the sieve.

Some mixtures are made up of a **solid** and a **liquid**. You can mix sand with water to make a mixture. You can separate the sand and water again using a **filter**.

Using a filter

Filter paper has very tiny holes in it that water can go through. If you have a mixture of sand and water, the sand grains are too big to go through the holes so they are trapped in the filter paper.

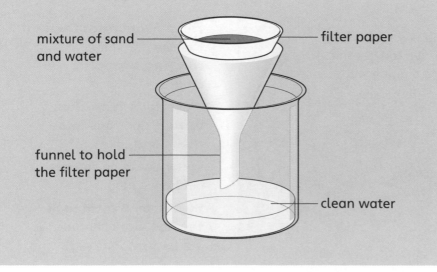

mixture of sand and water ——— ——— filter paper

funnel to hold the filter paper ———

——— clean water

What happens when solids dissolve?

Some solids dissolve in water. Sugar is a solid. If you mix sugar and water the sugar seems to disappear. You cannot see it any more, but you can tell that it is still there because the water tastes sweet. The mixture of sugar and water is called a solution. When a solid dissolves it breaks up into very tiny pieces. The pieces are so small that they can go through the holes in filter paper, so you cannot separate the solid from the water by filtering.

Your cup of tea

A tea bag is a filter. When you pour boiling water onto a tea bag, some of the substances in the tea leaves dissolve in the water and turn it brown. The dissolved substances can go through the small holes in the tea bag. The tea leaves are too big to fit through the holes, so they are trapped in the tea bag.

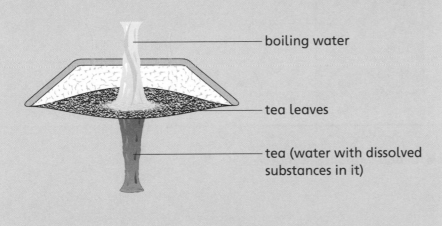

— boiling water

— tea leaves

— tea (water with dissolved substances in it)

Melting and **dissolving** are not the same thing!
A material will **melt** when it is heated.
Dissolving happens when a **liquid** is mixed with a solid that dissolves. There are two different substances mixed together in a solution.

Test yourself!

1 What is a sieve?

2 Why is a sieve useful for separating sand and peas?

3 How does a filter work when you use it to separate sand and water?

4 Why can't you use a filter to separate sugar and water?

Remember

A **mixture** is **different things jumbled together**.

You can use a **sieve** to **separate things of different sizes**.

You can use a **filter** to **separate a solid from a liquid**.

Some solids **dissolve** in water. You **cannot separate them from water** using a filter.

More about dissolving

Have you ever tried to dissolve sugar lumps in cold water? It takes a long time for the sugar to dissolve. Aisha, Matt and Donna decided to do some experiments to find out how to make sugar dissolve faster.

Aisha's experiment

Aisha wanted to find out if stirring helps sugar to dissolve. She put a spoonful of sugar into a beaker of water and measured how long it took to dissolve. Then she did the same thing again, but this time she stirred the water. She used the same amount of water and sugar each time to make sure her test was fair. Aisha used a bar chart to show her results, because she could describe the factor that she had changed in words – 'stirring' and 'not stirring'.

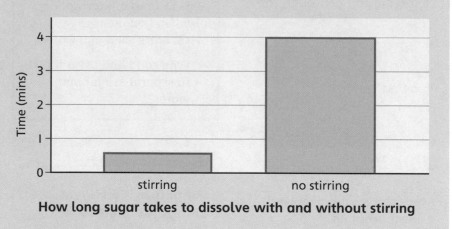

How long sugar takes to dissolve with and without stirring

Matt's experiment

Matt investigated the size of the pieces of sugar. He used caster sugar (which has very small grains), normal sugar and sugar lumps. The bar chart shows his results.

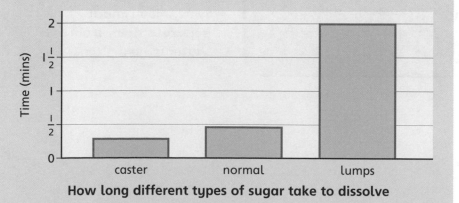

How long different types of sugar take to dissolve

Matt used a bar chart to show his results, because he could describe the sizes of the pieces in words – 'caster sugar', 'normal sugar' and 'sugar lumps'.

Donna's experiment

Donna wanted to find out if hot water would dissolve sugar faster than cold water. She used water at five different temperatures to find out the effect of temperature on the dissolving process. The graph shows her results.

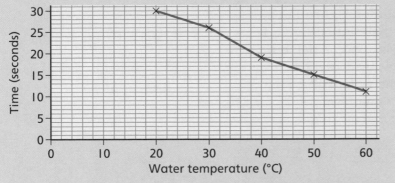

How long sugar takes to dissolve at different temperatures.

Donna used a line graph to show her results, because there are numbers between her measurements that mean something. For example, she could have used water at 35°C, and she would have found that the sugar took 22 seconds to dissolve.

After finishing their experiments, Aisha, Matt and Donna got together to discuss their results. They concluded that you can make sugar dissolve faster by:

• stirring the water
• using smaller pieces
• using hot water.

How much will dissolve?

Paul heard about the experiments that Aisha, Matt and Donna had carried out and started to think some more about how a solid dissolves. The next morning he put six spoonfuls of sugar in his cup of hot coffee. He stirred it for a minute, but he still had some pieces of sugar left at the bottom of the cup that did not dissolve. He realised that only a certain amount of a solid will dissolve in a liquid.

You can dissolve more solid if you have more liquid. For example, if you can dissolve 2 spoonfuls of sugar in 50cm³ of water, you can dissolve 4 spoonfuls in 100cm³ of water. The more water you have, the more sugar you can dissolve.

Some materials dissolve better than others. For instance, you might be able to dissolve 2 scoops of salt in a glass of water, but you would be able to dissolve about 12 scoops of sugar in the same amount of water.

You can find out more about graphs and charts on pages 85 and 86.

Test yourself!

1 Write down three ways to make sugar dissolve faster.

2 How can you make more sugar dissolve in water?

★3 What should Donna have kept the same to make her test fair?

Remember

You can make **dissolving happen faster** by **stirring, using hot water**, or **using smaller pieces**.

The **more water** you have, the **more sugar you can dissolve** in it.

Separating solutions

When a **solid** begins to dissolve in water it breaks up into very tiny pieces. These pieces are small enough to go through the holes in **filter** paper. This is why you cannot use filtering to separate sugar from water, or salt from water.

How to separate a solution of salty water

You can separate the different parts of a **solution** by heating it, which speeds up **evaporation**. The water in the solution evaporates, and the solid is left behind. For instance, if you have a pan of salty water, you can heat it until all the water has evaporated. The salt that was dissolved in the water will be left behind in the pan. If you want to get pure water from the solution you have to trap the **water vapour** and make it condense again.

Water vapour has condensed on the lid. This water is pure water with no salt in it.

salty water

You can also get the salt out of salty water by leaving it to evaporate, but it will take much longer for all the water to evaporate if you do not heat it.

Rain is formed when sea water evaporates and then condenses again in the air. Sea water is salty, but rain water is not, because the salt gets left behind when the water evaporates. You can find out more about the water cycle on page 50.

Test yourself!

1 Why can't you use filter paper to separate a mixture of salt and water?

2 How can you get salt from salty water?

3 How can you get pure water from salty water?

Remember

When a **solid dissolves**, the **particles are tiny**, so you **cannot use a filter to separate them**.

You can **separate a solid from a solution** by **letting the water evaporate**, leaving the solid behind.

You can get **pure water** by catching the water vapour and **condensing it**.

Reversible and irreversible changes

Reversible changes

Some materials change when you heat them. For instance, if you heat ice it will **melt** and change into **liquid** water. This is a **reversible change** because you can change the water back into ice by cooling it down until it freezes. Ice and water are both the same material, but each is in a different **state**. You can find out more about changing states on pages 46 to 49.

If you put salt into a glass of water the salt will **dissolve**. You can get the salt back by letting the water evaporate. The **evaporation** of the water leaves the salt behind. Dissolving is a reversible change. You can find out more about dissolving on pages 53 to 56.

You can also change materials by cooling them down. If you cool **water vapour**, it condenses and forms liquid water. This is a reversible change, because you can easily change the liquid water back into water vapour. Most changes caused by cooling are reversible.

Irreversible changes

Some changes are not reversible so we call them **irreversible** changes. If you bake a cake, the **mixture** of flour, eggs, butter and sugar changes into cake. The cake is a new material. You cannot get the raw eggs or flour back again. Cooking food is an example of an **irreversible change**.

Test yourself!

1 Write down three examples of reversible changes.

2 Write down one example of an irreversible change.

Remember

Changes of state and **dissolving** are **reversible** changes.

Cooking food is an **irreversible** change.

New materials are formed as a result of **irreversible changes**.

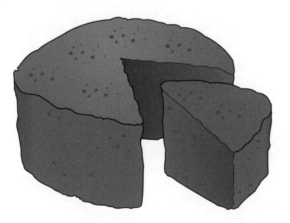

You cannot change this...

...back into this!

Irreversible changes

Irreversible changes caused by cooking

When you cook an egg, the clear, runny liquid changes into a white solid. The white solid is a new material. Cooking an egg causes an irreversible change. You cannot change the solid back into a runny liquid so you cannot reverse this change.

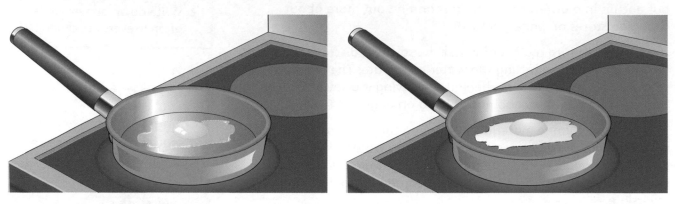

Irreversible changes caused by mixing substances

Some irreversible changes happen without heating.

Mixing concrete

Concrete is used to make buildings and paths. You can make concrete by mixing cement with gravel (small stones) and water. When the concrete dries it goes hard. The dried concrete is a new material – you cannot get the cement, gravel and water back again. This is an irreversible change.

Using baking powder

Baking powder helps cakes to rise. If you mix some baking powder with water you will see that the mixture 'fizzes'. Part of the baking powder has turned into a gas, which makes bubbles. The gas is a new material, so this is an irreversible change.

Irreversible changes caused by burning

Some materials **burn** when you heat them. **Burning** causes irreversible change.

Burning wood for warmth

You can burn wood to keep you warm. The burning logs give off heat, and form an invisible gas. Ash is left after all the logs have burnt. The logs have changed into ash and invisible gases. New materials have been made, so burning is an irreversible change.

Wood burns...   ...and turns into ash.

Burning gas as a fuel

Natural gas is used to cook food or to keep homes warm. It produces invisible gases when it burns.

Lots of materials in your home can burn if they are heated. Sometimes a fire starts accidentally. Fires can cause bad burns, which may even kill someone. Some materials give off poisonous gases when they burn, and breathing in the smoke and gases can also kill people.

Test yourself!

1 Write down two examples of irreversible changes that happen without heating.

2 How can you tell that burning wood is an irreversible change?

3 Write down two safety rules to help to prevent fires at home.

★4 Describe the changes that happen to a candle when it burns, and say if they are reversible or irreversible changes.

Remember

A change is **irreversible** if **new materials** are made.

A change is **usually irreversible** if a **gas** is made.

Burning is an **irreversible** change.

A **fire can harm people** if they **get burnt**, or if they breathe in **poisonous gases**.

Three rules for preventing fires

- **Never** play with matches
- **Never** leave clothes or toys near heaters or fires
- **Always** unplug electrical things when you have finished using them

Electricity – be safe!

Electricity is very useful. We use it to light up our homes, and to make things like TVs, computers and washing machines work.

Using mains electricity

Useful machines that use electricity are called **appliances**, and they need a lot of electricity. They have to be plugged into **sockets** in the wall, which provide mains electricity. The electricity that comes through the mains is powerful enough to kill you if you touch it.

Using batteries

Smaller things, like torches, personal stereos and mobile phones, do not need so much electricity to work. They use electricity from batteries. A battery is much safer to use because the electricity it provides is not powerful enough to harm you.

Be safe!

You can use mains electricity safely if you follow the simple rules shown in the poster below.

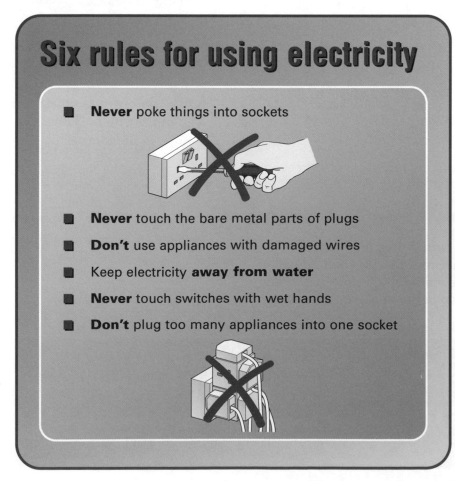

Six rules for using electricity

- **Never** poke things into sockets

- **Never** touch the bare metal parts of plugs
- **Don't** use appliances with damaged wires
- Keep electricity **away from water**
- **Never** touch switches with wet hands
- **Don't** plug too many appliances into one socket

Test yourself!

1. a) Write down the names of two appliances that use mains electricity.
   b) Why do these appliances need to use mains electricity?

2. List three things that use batteries.

3. Why are batteries safer than mains electricity?

4. Write down five rules for using electricity safely.

Remember

Mains electricity can kill you.

Batteries are **safe to use** because they **do not provide very much electricity**.

Keep safe by following the **safety rules** for using electricity.

Electrical circuits

There is a complete circuit inside everything that uses electricity. A circuit is made up of several different components, for example:

- a source of electricity, such as a battery
- a switch
- metal wires, covered in plastic
- a light bulb, if light is required.

The diagram below shows a simple circuit.

A simple circuit

The **battery** provides the electricity. A wire must be connected to each end of the battery.

The wire is covered in **plastic**. Plastic is an **insulator**, so electricity will not flow through it.

The **bulb** is a **component** that makes light. It is not working here because there is a gap in the circuit.

The inside of the wire is made of **metal**. Metal is a good **conductor** of electricity.

The **switch** controls the circuit. The circuit is not working because the switch is open. There is a gap in the circuit, so electricity cannot flow.

When you press the switch, there is a complete loop of wire for the electricity to flow around. The bulb lights up.

Other circuit components include:

- **buzzers**, which make a noise
- **motors**, which spin around.

Electricity will only flow if there is a complete looped pathway for it to flow around.

Test yourself!

1 a) Why are the insides of wires made of metal?
  b) Why are the outsides of wires made of plastic?

2 Why won't the bulbs work in these circuits?

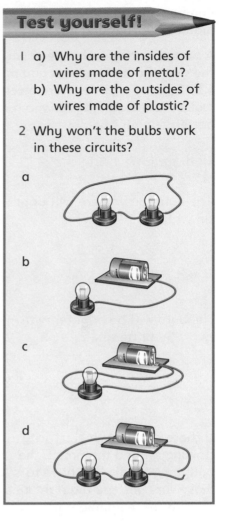

a

b

c

d

Remember

Electricity needs a **complete circuit** to flow around.

Switches work by **closing a gap** in the circuit.

Batteries, bulbs, buzzers, switches and **motors** are all **components**.

Changing components

Components are parts of an electrical circuit. Batteries, bulbs, motors, switches and buzzers are all components.

A battery provides the electricity in a circuit. The voltage written on the side of a battery tells you how much electricity it provides. A 4.5V battery provides more electricity than a 1.5V battery. You can make more electricity flow in a circuit by using more than one battery.

Adding more batteries

The bulb shown here will light up with a 1.5V battery.

1.5V

The bulb will be brighter with two 1.5V batteries.

1.5V   1.5V

If there is too much electricity flowing around the circuit, the bulb may break. You have to make sure you use the right kind of bulb for the amount of electricity in the circuit.

4.5V   4.5V

Adding more bulbs

You can change the brightness of bulbs by putting more bulbs in the circuit.

This bulb is bright.

1.5V   1.5V

If you put another bulb in, the electricity is shared between the bulbs so they are not as bright.

1.5V   1.5V

The above examples show that you can make bulbs brighter by:

• using more batteries
• using fewer bulbs.

Test yourself!

1 How can you tell how much electricity a battery will provide?

2 How can you make the bulbs in a circuit dimmer?

3 What might happen if you put too many batteries into a circuit?

★4 Explain two ways in which you can make the bulbs in this circuit brighter.

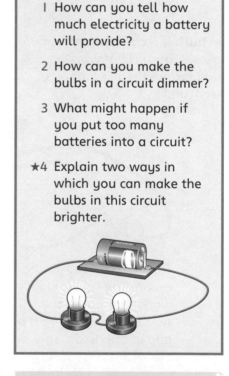

Remember

You can provide **more electricity** by using **more batteries**, or by using batteries with a **higher voltage**.

If you use **too many** batteries, the bulbs may **break**.

If you put **more bulbs** in a circuit, the bulbs will be **dimmer**.

Thin wires

You can change the brightness of bulbs in a circuit by changing the number of bulbs. If you put more bulbs into the circuit, the bulbs are dimmer. This is because it is more difficult for the electricity to flow through them all, so less electricity flows through the circuit. Bulbs are dimmer when there is less electricity flowing. You can also make bulbs dimmer by putting a piece of thin wire into the circuit. This is shown by the experiment described below.

Poppy's experiment

Poppy did an experiment to find out if the length and the thickness of the wire made a difference to the brightness of the bulbs.

1   First she tried a long wire.

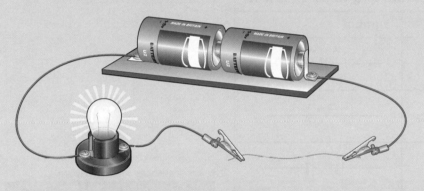

2   Then she used a shorter piece of the same wire. She used the same battery and bulb, to make sure her test was a fair test. She found that the bulb was brightest when the wire was short.

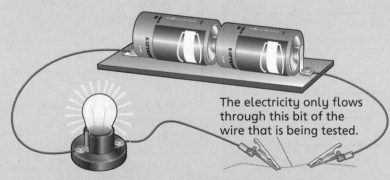

The electricity only flows through this bit of the wire that is being tested.

3   Then Poppy used a thick piece of wire, and then she used a thin piece of wire. The bulb was brightest when she used the thick wire.

Poppy found that:
*   the **shorter** the wire, the **brighter** the bulbs
*   the **thicker** the wire, the **brighter** the bulbs.

Poppy's experiment shows that it is easier for electricity to flow through short, thick wires than long, thin ones. More electricity will flow around the circuit, and the bulbs will be brighter.

Test yourself!

1   What happens to the brightness of a bulb if you add another bulb to the circuit?

2   Is it easier for electricity to flow through a thin wire or a thick wire?

3   If you put a long piece of wire into a circuit, will the bulbs get brighter or dimmer?

4   What did Poppy have to keep the same in her second experiment (step 3) to make sure her test was fair?

Remember

Adding bulbs or wires makes it more **difficult for electricity to flow** in a circuit.

If it is difficult for electricity to flow, less of it will flow round the circuit and bulbs will be **dimmer**.

It is **harder** for electricity to flow through **long, thin wires** than through **short, thick wires**.

Drawing circuits

We can use symbols to draw an electrical circuit. A symbol is a shape that represents something else. It is easier to draw a circuit using symbols than it is to draw pictures of the components.

It is easier to draw this...   ...than this.

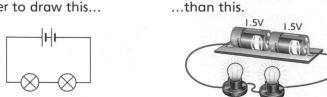

So that everyone can understand circuit diagrams, we always use the same symbol for each component. The symbols you need to know are shown in the table below.

Circuit diagrams – the eight symbols you need to know		
Name	**Picture**	**Symbol**
cell		+ |⊢ −
wire		
battery		
open switch		
closed switch		
bulb		⊗
motor		(M)
buzzer		

The proper scientific name for this is a **cell**.

A **battery** is two or more cells used together

Remember

We use **symbols** to draw **circuits**.

You need to **learn** all the **symbols on this page**.

Magnets and magnetic materials

The effect of magnets on each other

A **magnet** can **attract** another magnet. If you hold two magnets close to each other, you can feel them pulling. If you turn one of the magnets round they will **repel** (push away from) each other.

Magnetic forces

The pushes and pulls between magnets are **forces**. We can use arrows to show forces.

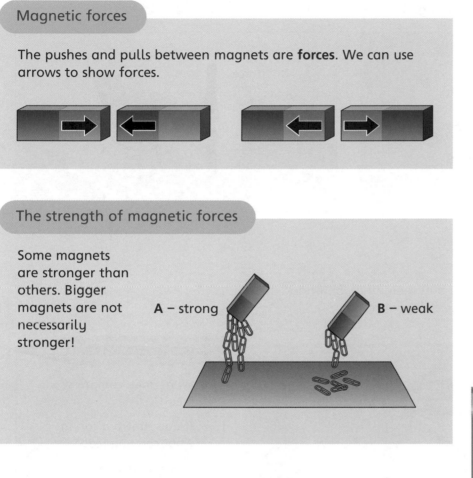

The strength of magnetic forces

Some magnets are stronger than others. Bigger magnets are not necessarily stronger!

A – strong   **B – weak**

Magnets and magnetic materials

A magnet can attract things made of **iron** because iron is a **magnetic material**. The force from a magnet lets you pick up things like paper clips or food cans that have iron in them.

Iron is a **magnetic material**, because it can be picked up by a magnet. Steel is a metal that is mainly made from iron, so it is also a magnetic material.

Not all metals are magnetic materials. For example, drinks cans are made from a kind of metal called aluminium, which is not a magnetic material. So you cannot pick up aluminium cans using a magnet. This is a useful idea for recycling, because you can easily separate steel and aluminium cans using a magnet.

Test yourself!

1 What does 'repel' mean?

2 Look at the picture of magnets A and B. How can you tell from the picture that magnet A is the strongest?

3 Write down the names of two magnetic materials.

★4 Describe how to separate aluminium and steel cans using a magnet.

Remember

Magnets can **attract** and **repel** each other.

Magnets can **attract magnetic materials** such as **iron**.

Springs

Springs are very useful. Springs are used in mattresses, armchairs, staplers and in some doors that shut on their own.

If you **compress** (squash) a spring, you can feel it pushing back on your hands. If you stretch a spring, you can feel it pulling back on your hands. The force from the spring is in the opposite direction to the force you are putting onto the spring.

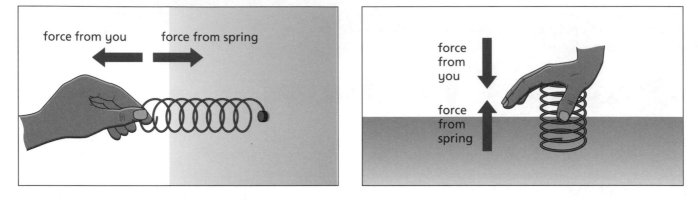

Using an elastic band as a spring

Elastic bands are like springs. If you pull them, they pull back. You can use an elastic band to make a toy car move.

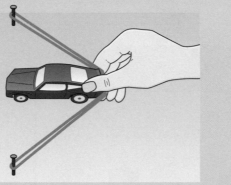

If you only pull the elastic band a little way, the car does not go very far. If you pull the elastic band a long way, the car will go further because the elastic band will put a bigger force on it. The further you stretch the elastic band, the harder it pulls back.

Springs are very useful for measuring forces. A **forcemeter** has a spring inside it. If you pull it gently the spring only stretches a little way. If you use a bigger force (pull harder) the spring stretches further. The units for measuring forces are **newtons (N)**.

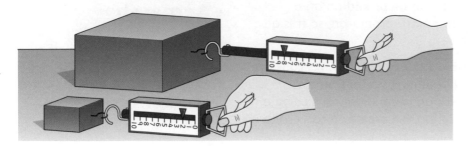

Test yourself!

1 What does 'compress' mean?

2 If you stretch a spring, what can you feel?

3 What is inside a forcemeter?

4 What are the units for measuring force?

Remember

The **force from a spring** is in the **opposite direction** to the force you put into it.

If you **pull** springs or elastic bands **further**, they **pull back harder**.

Springs are used in **forcemeters**.

The **units** for forces are **newtons (N)**.

Gravity and weight

Gravity is a **force** that pulls everything downward towards the Earth. The weight of something is the force of the Earth's gravity pulling on it. Weight is a **force**, so it is measured in newtons **(N)**.

Using a forcemeter

You can use a forcemeter to weigh things. This forcemeter is being used to measure the weight of the apple. The weight of the apple pulls on the spring inside the forcemeter and stretches it. The pointer is attached to the spring, and shows you the weight.

This forcemeter is weighing the mug. The mug is heavier than the apple, so the spring in the forcemeter stretches further.

Comparing gravity on the Earth and the Moon

All objects attract each other. You are pulling on the Earth at the same time as the Earth is pulling on you.

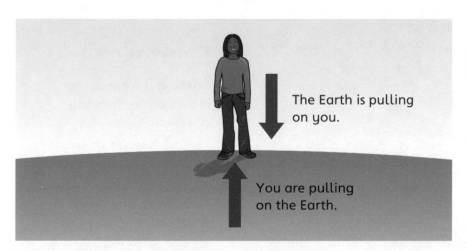

The Earth is pulling on you.

You are pulling on the Earth.

There is also gravity on the Moon. The force of gravity is smaller on the Moon than it is on the Earth, so things do not weigh as much. When astronauts visited the Moon they could jump a long way, because the Moon's gravity is weak.

Test yourself!

1 What is gravity?

2 What is weight?

3 How can you measure the weight of a book?

★4 If you could visit the Moon, would it be easier or more difficult to lift a large rock than it would be on Earth? Explain your answer.

Remember

Gravity is a **force** that **pulls things towards each other**.

The **force of gravity** on you is **your weight**.

Weight is measured in **newtons (N)**.

Gravity is **less** on the **Moon**.

Friction

Friction is a force that slows down moving objects. Look at the picture below. There is friction between the box and the table. You can measure the amount of friction using a **forcemeter**.

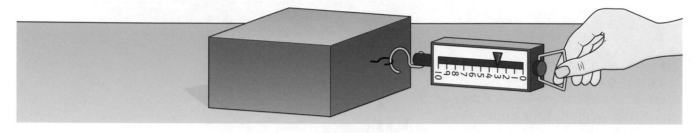

It is easiest to pull the block on a smooth surface. Smooth surfaces have the least friction, and rough surfaces have the most friction.

Is friction useful?

Friction can be useful. For example, friction between the road and tyres stops cars and bicycles skidding on the road. Roads have rough surfaces to increase the friction.

Sometimes you do not want much friction, such as on a playground slide. Slides have very smooth surfaces so that friction is low and you can go fast!

Slowing down

Objects are slowed down when they move through water and air. **Water resistance** and **air resistance** are both kinds of friction.

Water resistance

Water resistance slows down things that are moving through water, such as boats and fish. Fish have a special smooth shape to reduce water resistance and let them swim fast.

Air resistance

Air resistance slows down things that are moving through the air. For example, parachutes have a large air resistance so they fall slowly. Birds have a smooth shape so that they have a low air resistance and can fly fast.

Remember

Friction is a **force** that **slows down moving objects**.

Friction is **least** when the surfaces are **smooth**.

Water resistance and **air resistance** are **kinds of friction**.

Water resistance and **air resistance** are **small** when things have **smooth shapes**.

Balanced forces

If you hold a football in your hand, the force from your hand is holding it up, and you can feel the **weight** of the football pulling down. The weight of the football is the same size as the force from your hand. The two forces are **balanced forces**, so the football does not move.

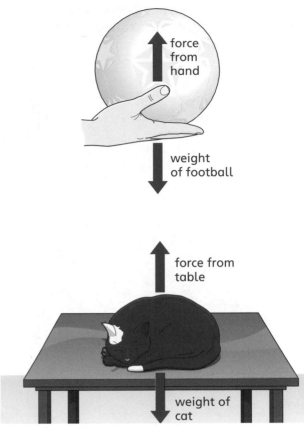

force from hand

weight of football

The cat in this picture is not moving. Its weight is pulling it down, but the force from the table is holding it up. The two forces are balanced. All **stationary** (still) objects have balanced forces acting on them.

force from table

weight of cat

Weighing things

We use ideas about balanced forces when we weigh things. Look at the diagram. The spring in the **forcemeter** stretches when you hang the mug on it. The more the spring stretches, the harder it pulls back. The mug stops moving down when the force from the spring is the same as the weight from the mug, and you can read the weight from the scale.

force from the spring

weight of the mug

Balanced forces can be horizontal, too. In this picture, the force from the baby is the same as the force from her mother, so she cannot move to reach the sweet.

force from baby

force from mother

Test yourself!

1 What are the forces on you when you stand on the floor?

2 Why isn't this dog moving?

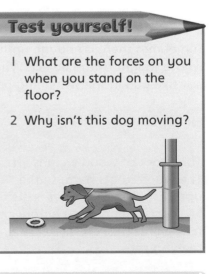

Remember

All **stationary objects** have **balanced forces** acting on them.

Upthrust

You can float in a swimming pool because a force from the water is holding you up. This force is called **upthrust**. You can find out about upthrust using a **forcemeter**.

Measuring upthrust

This box weighs 8N.

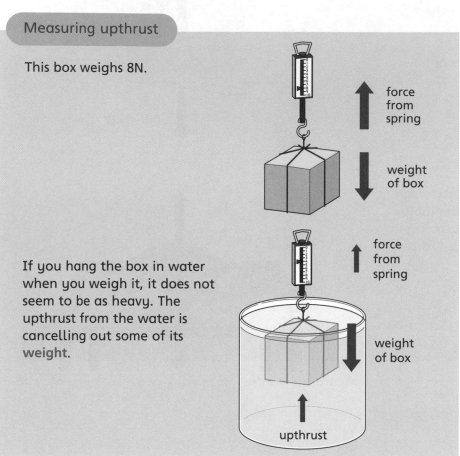

force from spring

weight of box

If you hang the box in water when you weigh it, it does not seem to be as heavy. The upthrust from the water is cancelling out some of its **weight**.

force from spring

weight of box

upthrust

Floating

Sometimes there is enough upthrust from the water to balance the whole weight of the object. When this happens, the object floats – just like you in the swimming pool.

Floating wood block

This block of wood weighs 5N. The wood floats because the upthrust from the water is also 5N, and is completely balancing its weight. The forcemeter is reading zero.

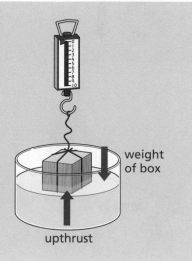

weight of box

upthrust

Test yourself!

1 What is upthrust?

2 a) This duck weighs 25N. What is the upthrust on it?

   b) The duckling weighs 2N. What is the upthrust on it?

★3 What is the upthrust on this box when it is in water?

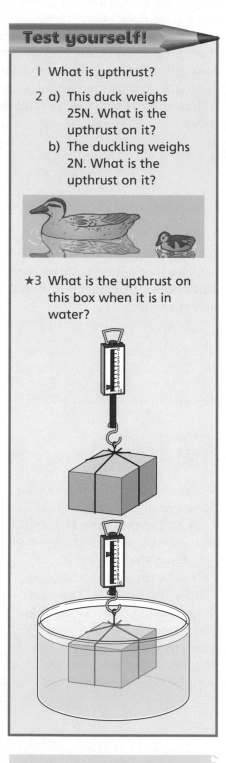

Remember

Upthrust is an **upwards force** from water.

Objects **float** when the **upthrust balances the weight**.

Light and seeing

We need light to see things. A **light source** is something that makes its own light. The Sun, light bulbs, candles and torches are all light sources. We see things when light from them goes into our eyes.

Most things do not make their own light. These things are not light sources. We can see them because light is reflected from them and goes into our eyes.

Never look at the sun
It can damage your eyes.

Light travels in straight lines

Light travels in straight lines, so we can show the direction light is travelling using a straight line with an arrow on it.

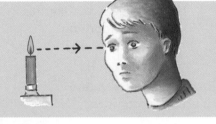

Remember – the light is travelling **from** the light source **to** your eyes, so make sure the arrow shows this when you draw a diagram!

Light can travel through some materials

Light can travel through **transparent** materials, such as glass.

Some materials are **translucent**, which means that light can go through them but you cannot see through them clearly. Bathroom windows are often made from translucent glass.

Light cannot travel through **opaque** materials such as wood or brick.

| transparent | translucent | opaque |

Test yourself!

1 What do the words 'transparent' and 'opaque' mean?

2 Draw a diagram to show how light travels from a light bulb to your eyes.

3 Why does a stick have a shadow on a sunny day?

Shadows

There is a **shadow** behind the stick in the picture, because light cannot go through or round the stick. Light travels in straight lines. It cannot go through opaque things, so opaque objects form shadows.

Remember

Light travels in **straight lines**.

We **see** things when **light goes into our eyes**.

Light **can** go through **transparent** objects but **not** through **opaque** ones.

Opaque objects can form **shadows**.

Changing shadows

You can investigate shadows by looking at the **shadow** of a stick at different times during the **day**.

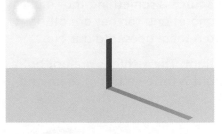

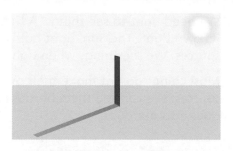

The shadow looks like this in the morning.

The shadow looks like this in the afternoon. The shadow has moved because, as the Earth turns on its axis, the Sun is in a different position in relation to the stick.

You can also experiment with shadows using a torch and two pieces of card. Use one of the pieces of card as a screen, as shown below.

Experimenting with shadows

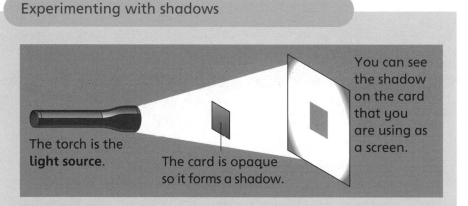

You can see the shadow on the card that you are using as a screen.

The torch is the **light source**.

The card is opaque so it forms a shadow.

If you move the screen further away from the torch, the shadow gets bigger.

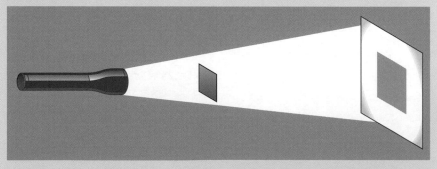

If you move the opaque card closer to the torch, the shadow gets bigger.

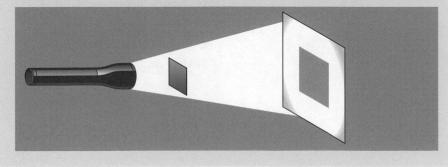

Test yourself!

1 Why does the shadow of a stick change during the day?

2 What apparatus do you need to investigate shadows in the classroom or at home?

★3 Describe two ways to make a shadow smaller.

Remember

Shadows move if the **light source moves**.

You can change the **size** of a shadow by **moving** the **light source** or the **opaque object**.

Shadows get bigger if the **light source is closer to the opaque object**.

Reflecting light

What is reflection?

Light can bounce off some materials. This is called **reflection**. Light coloured, shiny surfaces reflect light very well. Dark, dull surfaces do not reflect light well.

Be safe on the roads

You can keep safe on the roads by wearing light coloured clothes, or special reflective clothes. These clothes will reflect light much better than dark clothes, and make it easier for car drivers to see you.

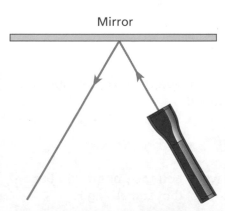

Mirrors

Mirrors are very good at reflecting light. You can see an **image** of yourself in a mirror.

Light changes direction when it hits a mirror. You can show how this happens in a diagram by drawing straight lines with arrows on them.

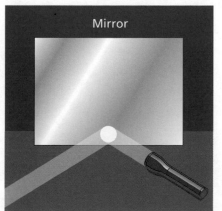

Mirror

An image in a mirror is not the same as a shadow. Your shadow is dark, and you can only see your shape. When you look at your image in a mirror you can see your face properly.

Test yourself!

1 Why should you wear light coloured clothes if you go out at night?

2 What is your reflection in a mirror called?

3 How can you show what happens to a beam of light when it hits a mirror?

Remember

Reflection happens when **light bounces off things**.

Light coloured, shiny materials are **best at reflecting light**.

Light **changes direction** when it is **reflected**.

Sound and vibrations

Making different sounds

Sounds are made when things **vibrate** (move backwards and forwards quickly). If you make a noise using a ruler, you can see that the ruler is vibrating.

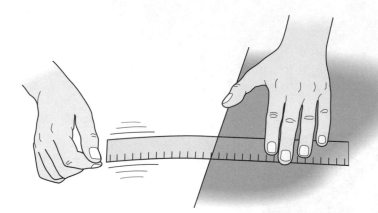

When you play a guitar, you pluck the strings and make them vibrate. The vibrating strings make the sound.

The skin of a drum vibrates when you hit it, and makes a sound.

When you blow into a recorder, the air inside the recorder vibrates. It is this vibrating air that makes a sound.

Making sounds using your voice

You cannot see anything vibrating when you talk, but if you put your fingers on your throat you can feel that something is vibrating inside you!

You can make lots of different sounds using your voice. The sounds that you make can be **loud** or **quiet**. You can also make high or low sounds. A high sound has a high **pitch**, and a low sound has a low pitch. You will learn more about loudness and pitch on pages 76 and 77.

How you hear sounds

You hear sounds when the vibrations travel to your ears. When your friends call out to you, the vibrations from their mouths travel through the air to your ears. Air is a **gas**. Sound can travel through gases.

If you put your ears under the water in the bath or at the swimming pool, you can still hear sounds. Water is a **liquid**, and sound can travel through liquids.

Sounds can also travel through a **solid**. If you are in a room with the doors and windows shut, you can still hear things that are happening outside. Sounds can travel through glass, bricks and wood.

Is there sound in space?

Sound cannot travel if there is nothing for it to travel through. Astronauts in space cannot talk directly to each other because there is no air for sound to travel through. Instead, they have to use radios to speak to one another.

Noise

Sometimes sounds are too loud. Some sounds, like lorries on the road outside, are annoying. Some sounds are so loud that they can damage our ears. Annoying sounds are sometimes called **noise**.

Too noisy!

You can cut down the amount of sound in a house by using soft materials like curtains and carpets. These materials **absorb** some of the vibrations, and make the sounds quieter.

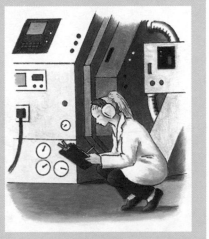

Sometimes you cannot stop things making sounds, so you have to protect your ears instead. This woman is working in a noisy factory. She is wearing special ear muffs to stop the loud noises damaging her ears.

Pitch and loudness

High and low

Musical instruments can make sounds with different **pitches**.

On a xylophone, the long bars make notes with a low **pitch**, and the short bars make notes with a high pitch.

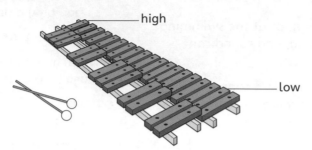

Small drums make higher pitched sounds than big drums. You can also make the pitch of a drum higher by tightening the skin.

Changing pitch when playing a guitar

When you play a guitar, you can change the length of the strings by putting your fingers on them. When you pluck a string it will **vibrate**.

This string will make a low pitched note.

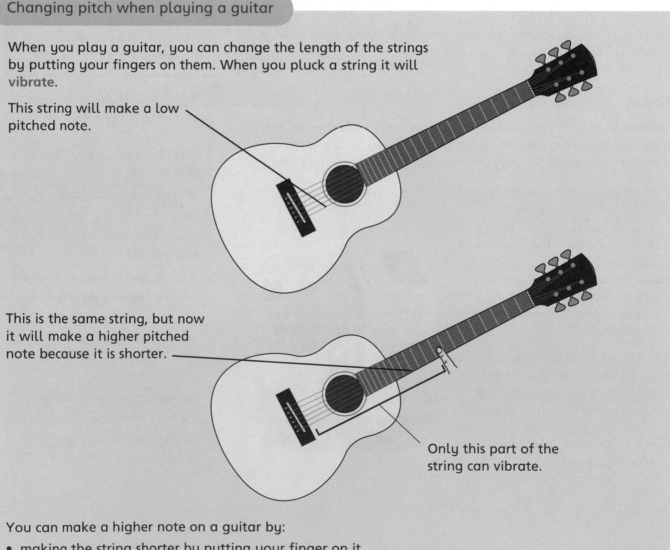

This is the same string, but now it will make a higher pitched note because it is shorter.

Only this part of the string can vibrate.

You can make a higher note on a guitar by:
• making the string shorter by putting your finger on it
• making the string tighter
• using a thinner string.

Changing pitch when playing a wind instrument

Some instruments make sounds because the air inside them is vibrating. These instruments are called wind instruments. The length of the air inside the instrument is called the **air column**. Long air columns make lower sounds than short ones. The longer the air column, the lower the **pitch**.

You can change the length of the air column in a trombone by moving the slide in and out.

This is the length of the air column that vibrates for a high note.

This is the length of the air column that vibrates for a low note.

Loud and soft

Musical instruments can make loud sounds or soft, quiet sounds. You can make loud sounds on drums by hitting them hard, and quiet sounds by hitting them gently. When you blow a recorder, you make loud sounds by blowing hard, and quiet sounds by blowing gently.

Test yourself!

1 How do you make a loud sound on a recorder?

2 How can you make a quiet sound on a drum?

3 How can you make a low pitched sound on a trombone?

★4 Write down three ways of making a low note on a guitar.

Remember

Longer or **bigger** instruments make **lower pitched sounds** than **shorter** or **smaller** ones.

You can increase the **pitch of a drum** by **tightening the skin**.

You can increase the **pitch of a guitar** by **tightening the string**, making it **shorter**, or using a **thinner** string.

You can increase the **pitch of a wind instrument** by making the **air column shorter**.

Earth, Sun and Moon

Earth

The Earth is the planet we live on. It is shaped like a **sphere**.

How do we know that the Earth is a sphere?

We know that the Earth is a sphere because astronauts have taken photographs of the Earth from space.

However, people knew that the Earth was a sphere even before astronauts went into space. Some of the **evidence** for this idea was:

- when ships sailed away, the bottom part of the ship disappeared first
- the shadow of the same object was a different length in different places
- ships had sailed all the way around the world without falling off the edge!

The Earth does not look like a sphere when we stand on it, because it is so big. You have to be a long way from the Earth before you can see that it is spherical.

The diameter of the Earth is nearly 13 000km.

Sun and Moon

The Sun and the Moon are also spheres. The Moon is smaller than the Earth. The Sun is much bigger than the Moon and the Earth, but it is also much further away, which is why the Sun and the Moon look about the same size.

If you draw the Sun to the same scale as used in the diagram above, it will be over 50 centimetres across and nearly 6 metres away.

Day and night

The Sun seems to move across the sky each day. However, the Sun is not really moving across the sky. The Earth is spinning. The Sun **seems** to move because we are standing on a spinning Earth.

You must **never** look at the Sun directly, because it could damage your eyes, but you can see how the Sun seems to move by looking at the shadow of a stick.

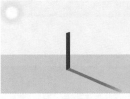

Morning – the Sun rises in the east

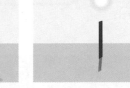

Midday – the Sun is above us

Evening – the Sun sets in the west

Our spinning planet

The diagrams below show why the Sun seems to be moving across the sky.

The Sun seems to be in the **east**.

The Earth has spun round a little, so now the Sun seems to be **above** you.

The Earth spins a bit more, and now the Sun seems to be in the **west**.

How long does it take the Earth to spin around?

The Earth spins round once every 24 hours.

It is **daytime** in the parts of the Earth facing towards the Sun.

It is **night-time** in the parts of the Earth facing away from the Sun.

It is daytime on this part of the Earth, because it is facing the Sun.

It is night on this part of the Earth, because it is facing away from the Sun.

Test yourself!

1 Does the Sun rise in the east or the west?

2 Why does the Sun seem to move across the sky?

3 How long does it take for the Earth to spin around once?

★4 Describe how the shadow of a stick changes during the day.

Remember

The Sun **rises in the east** and **sets in the west**.

The Sun **seems to move** because **the Earth is spinning**.

It is **daytime** when our part of the Earth is **facing the Sun**.

Orbits

The Earth spins round, which is why we have **day** and **night** – this is explained on page 79. The Earth is also moving around the Sun. It takes one **year** for the Earth to go around the Sun once. There are 365 days in a year. The path that the Earth takes around the Sun is its **orbit**.

The Earth really takes $365\frac{1}{4}$ days to orbit the Sun once. We can't have a quarter of a day, so every four years we have a leap year, which has 366 days in it.

The Moon's orbit

The Moon orbits around the Earth. This means that the Moon moves around the Earth. It takes the Moon 28 days to go around the Earth once.

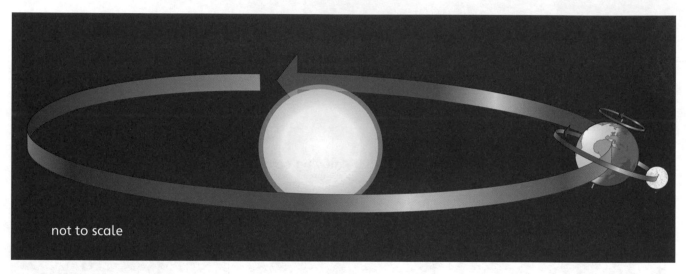

not to scale

Phases of the Moon

The shape of the Moon seems to change as it moves around the Earth. The different shapes are called **phases of the Moon**. The Moon does not make its own light. We see the Moon because it reflects light from the Sun. It reflects different amounts of light at different times in its orbit – this is why its shape seems to change.

Full Moon   New Moon

Test yourself!

1   How long does it take the Earth to go around the Sun once?

2   How long does it take the Moon to go around the Earth once?

3   How can we see the Moon?

Remember

The Earth moves around the Sun.

It takes **365 days**, or **one year**, to **go around once**.

The **Moon goes around the Earth** once every **28 days**.

Questions to investigate

Scientists investigate things to find out how the world works. They do this by asking questions and then trying to find the answers to those questions. Not all questions can be investigated scientifically.

Do apples taste nice?

This is not a good question for an investigation, because it cannot be answered scientifically. The answer depends on people's opinions. Think about how you could change the question in order to investigate it.

Do most people think that apples taste nice?

This is a much better question than 'Do apples taste nice?' Now you can do a survey to find out how many people like the taste of apples, and how many do not.

Which is the best material for clothes?

This is not a good question, because it depends on what you want the clothes for. The best material for a raincoat would not be the same as the best material for your disco clothes! It would be better to change the question to say 'Which materials are waterproof?' You could then predict which materials you think might be waterproof, and design an investigation to test whether your predictions are correct.

Which animals live in the wood?

This is a good question, because you can go to the wood and look for different animals.

Which animals live the longest?

You cannot investigate this question directly yourself, but you can look up the answer in books about nature. This is a good question.

How can you make a parachute fall more slowly?

This is a good question. Think about possible factors that might slow the parachute down. Now you can design an experiment to find out the answer.

Test yourself!

I Can these questions be investigated scientifically? Explain your answers.
   a) Are flowers pretty?
   b) How much air is in soil?
   c) Which surfaces give the most friction?
   d) Which is the best month of the year?

Remember

Scientists **ask questions** that can be **investigated scientifically**.

Fair tests

When you are doing a scientific experiment, you must make sure that your test is a **fair test**. This means that you must only change one **factor** at a time.

Dawn's experiment

Dawn did an experiment to find out how much **friction** there was on different surfaces. She did two tests.

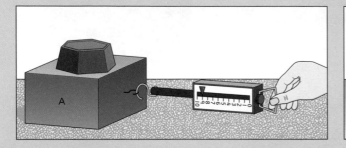
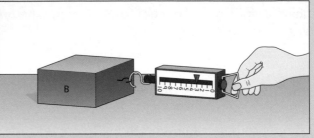

It was hardest to pull block A. This was not a very good experiment, because Dawn cannot tell whether the friction was increased by the rough surface, the size of the box or the **weight** on the box.

Dawn's test was not a fair test because she changed several factors at the same time.

Jacob's experiment

Jacob also wanted to find out about friction. First, he made a list of all the **factors** that could affect the amount of friction. This is Jacob's list:

> These things could affect the amount of friction:
> - the size of the box
> - the weight on the box
> - the roughness of the surface.

Jacob decided to test the roughness of the surface. He kept the other factors the same.

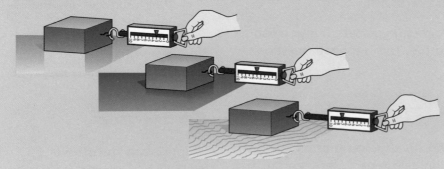

Jacob's test was a fair test, because he only changed one factor.

Remember

Factors are the things that could **affect your experiment**.

In a **fair test**, you can only change **one factor at a time**.

Measuring and units

In most scientific investigations you need to measure things. Sometimes you just need to count things (such as the number of woodlice under a stone), but you usually need to use equipment to measure things.

When you measure something, it is very important to include the **units**. Saying that a worm is 7 long does not really mean anything – you could mean 7 millimetres or 7 metres!

The table shows some of the measuring instruments you might use in scientific investigations and the units to use.

Measurement	Instrument		Units	
length	ruler or tape measure		metres centimetres millimetres	m cm mm
temperature	thermometer		degrees Celsius	°C
force	forcemeter		newtons	N
time	stopwatch		minutes seconds	m s
capacity (volume)	measuring cylinder		centimetres cubed*	cm³

* 1cm³ is the same capacity as 1ml – some measuring cylinders are marked in cm³, and some in ml, but they both mean the same.

Measuring temperature

When you are measuring temperature, remember that a thermometer reads the temperature of whatever it is standing in.

This thermometer is measuring the temperature of the water.

This thermometer is **not** measuring the temperature of the water – it is measuring the temperature of the air above the water!

Remember

When you write down a **measurement**, always **include the units**.

Tables

A table is a way of presenting information that is easy to understand. You need to draw a table ready for your results before you start an experiment, so that you have somewhere to write down your measurements.

Amesh's experiment

Amesh did an experiment to find out how far an elastic band stretched when he hung different weights on it. This is the table he drew for his results.

This is what Amesh was changing, so it goes in the first column.

These are the weights that Amesh will be hanging on his elastic band.

This is what Amesh will be measuring.

Always put the units in.

This will be the length of the elastic band before Amesh adds any weights.

Use a ruler to draw the straight lines in the table.

Weight on elastic band (N)	Length of elastic band (cm)
0	
1	
2	
3	
4	
5	

Emily's experiment

Emily did an experiment to find out how much of different substances would **dissolve** in water. This is the table she drew for her results.

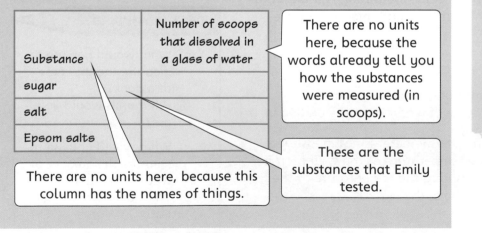

Substance	Number of scoops that dissolved in a glass of water
sugar	
salt	
Epsom salts	

There are no units here, because the words already tell you how the substances were measured (in scoops).

These are the substances that Emily tested.

There are no units here, because this column has the names of things.

Remember

Put the thing you are **changing** in the **first column of the table**.

Include **units** for any numbers in the table.

Make your table **neat** – use a **ruler** to draw straight lines.

Bar charts

A **bar chart** is a way of showing your results. It can help you to see patterns in the results.

You can use a bar chart to show your results if one of the things you have studied can be described in words. If your results are two sets of numbers, you need to show your results using a **line graph**. You can find out more about line graphs on page 86.

Look at the two experiments described on page 84. Amesh can use a line graph to show his results, because he has two sets of numbers in his table. Emily can use a bar chart to show her results because one of the things she studied can be described in words.

Emily's results

Substance	Number of scoops that dissolved in a glass of water
sugar	9
salt	3
Epsom salts	2

Emily's bar chart

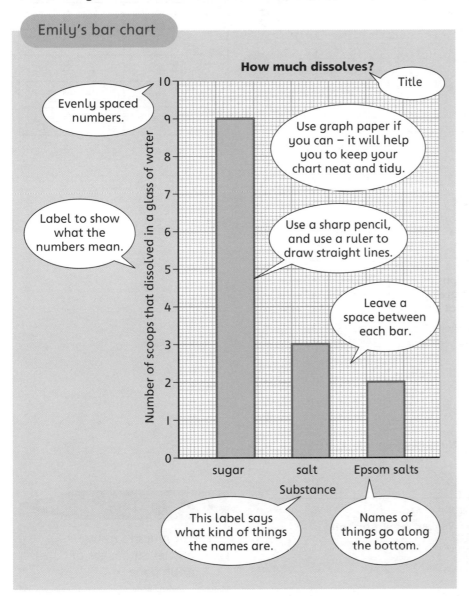

Evenly spaced numbers.

Title

Use graph paper if you can – it will help you to keep your chart neat and tidy.

Label to show what the numbers mean.

Use a sharp pencil, and use a ruler to draw straight lines.

Leave a space between each bar.

This label says what kind of things the names are.

Names of things go along the bottom.

Test yourself!

1 Draw a bar chart to show the results of Jacob's friction experiment (see page 82). The results are shown in the table below.

Jacob's results

Surface	Force needed (N)
polished	1
painted	3
rough wood	9

Remember

Use a **bar chart** to present your results when **one of the things you have investigated** can be **described in words**.

Line graphs

You can use a line graph to show your results when you have **two sets of numbers**. Line graphs are useful because they can help you to make predictions.

Amesh's line graph

These are Amesh's results from his experiment on elastic bands → (page 84).

This is the line graph that Amesh drew to show his results. ↓

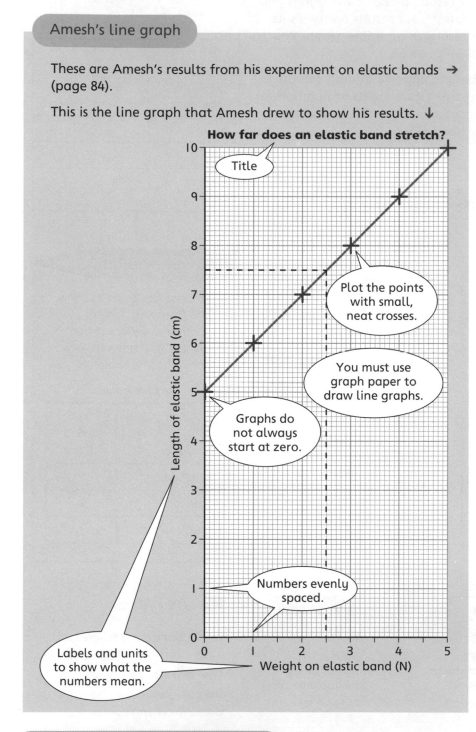

Amesh's results

Weight on elastic band (N)	Length of elastic band (cm)
0	5
1	6
2	7
3	8
4	9
5	10

Test yourself!

1 Plot Amesh's results (above) on a piece of graph paper.

Using a line graph for predictions

Amesh can use his line graph to predict how long the elastic band would be if he hung a different **weight** on it. The dotted line on the graph shows you how to use it to **predict** the length of the elastic band if Amesh hangs a 2.5N weight on it.

Remember

You can draw a **line graph** when your results are **two sets of numbers**.

Conclusions and evaluations

Conclusions

Your **conclusion** is what you have found out in an investigation. Before you write down your conclusion you need to see if you can find any patterns in your results. It is usually easier to see patterns if you draw a bar chart or line graph to show your results.

Emily's conclusions

Look at the bar chart showing Emily's results. Emily's conclusion could be:

- 'Sugar dissolves the best.'

  > This is OK.

- 'You can dissolve a lot more sugar in water than salt or Epsom salts.'

  > This is better, because it also mentions the other substances that Emily tested.

- 'I can dissolve about three times as much sugar as salt in the same amount of water.'

  > This is even better, because Emily has said how much more sugar will dissolve.

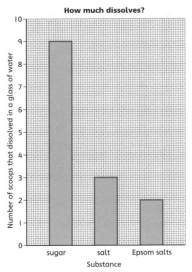

Amesh's conclusions

Look at the line graph of Amesh's results. Amesh could make these conclusions:

- 'The elastic band is 10cm long when 5N is hanging from it.'

  > This is not very good – it is only saying what is in the table.

- 'A big **weight** makes the elastic band long.'

  > This is better.

- 'The bigger the weight, the longer the elastic band.'

  > This is best – always try to write your conclusion using comparing words (these are often words that end in 'er', for example, smaller, shorter, heavier, lighter)

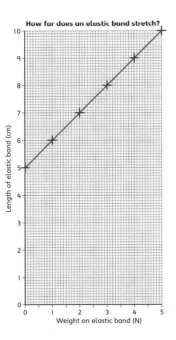

Evaluations

Your **evaluation** is where you say how good your results were, or whether you could do the investigation better if you had time to do it again. You should ask yourself these questions when you are evaluating your investigation.

- Did I do a **fair test**?
- Were my measuring instruments accurate enough?
- Have I got enough results?
- Do any of my results look wrong? Should I do any measurements again?

Remember

Your **conclusion** says **what you found out** in your investigation.

Your **evaluation** says **how good your results were**.

Answers

Page 5

1 Nutrition, respiration, movement, growth and reproduction.
2 They eat plants or other animals.
3 They make it using sunlight.
4 By making seeds.

Pages 6–7

1 To cut and chew food.
2 Incisors, canines and molars.
3 To grind up grass.
4 The first set of teeth.
5 Brushing them, not eating sweet things, not having fizzy drinks, eating foods like apples or carrots, going to the dentist.
6 Long canine teeth and pointed molars, to help them to kill animals and tear up the meat.

Pages 8–9

1 To grow, to stay healthy and for energy.
2 Meat, fish, milk, cheese, eggs, beans, lentils.
3 Bread, pasta, rice and cereals; milk, cheese, butter, oil and meat; sweets, cakes, biscuits and fizzy drinks.
4 Fruit and vegetables.
5 A diet that gives your body all the things it needs in the right amounts.
6 She should eat more fruit and vegetables, and more pasta, bread etc., so she gets enough food for health and energy.

Page 10

1 To protect parts of your body, to support you, and to let you move.
2 Protects the brain.
3 It has joints, which let arms and legs bend.

Page 11

1 To move your bones.
2
a) A
b) It will relax and get longer.

Pages 12–13

1 Food.
2 Heart.
3 Arteries.
4 The number of heart beats per minute.

5 Your table should show 'low' for all the things that you do sitting down or lying down. It should show 'medium' for when you are standing up or walking around slowly, and it should show 'high' when you are running around.

Pages 14–15

1 Eat a balanced diet and get exercise.
2 Substances that change the way your body works.
3
a) Something a drug does to you that you do not want.
b) Feeling sleepy after taking a medicine to stop you feeling travel sick.
4 They make people feel good.
5 Alcohol can make you feel ill the next day, and it can harm your body. Tobacco can damage your heart and lungs.
6 You could be hit by a car whose driver had been drinking. You could breathe in the smoke from other people's cigarettes.

Page 16

1 Baby, child, adolescent, adult.
2 Nine months.
3 18

Page 17

1 To make food.
2 To support the plant and carry water.
3 To hold the plant in the soil and to take in water.
4
a) Plant A
b) It has more light and it has space to grow.

Page 18

1 Water, air and light.
2 Water and nutrients.
3 To make sure there are enough nutrients to keep plants healthy.
4 To support them in windy weather. A big plant also needs more water, so it needs bigger roots to take in the water.
5 Small, shallow roots, because grass plants are small.

Page 19

1 Pollen is taken from one plant to another.
2 Pollen joins with an ovum.
3 Seeds are spread out away from the plant.
4 Seeds start to grow.

Page 20

1 The stamens.
2 The ovary.
3 To attract insects.
4 Protect the flower when it is a bud.

Page 21

1 To attract insects.
2 To attract insects.
3 A seed.
4 Pollination is when pollen travels between one plant and another. Fertilisation is when pollen that has already landed on a plant joins an ovum.

Page 22

1 So they get enough light, air, water, nutrients and space to grow.
2 Wind, water, animals, or explosion.
3 So they can be carried away by the wind.
4 So animals want to eat them.

Page 23

1 When seeds start to grow.
2 Water and warmth.
3 Plant some seeds with enough water and warmth, but keep them in the dark. If they start to grow, it shows that seeds do not need light to germinate.

Pages 24–25

1 To make it easier to think about them.
2 Plants can make their own food, and animals cannot.
3
a) Fulmar.
b) Arctic tern.
c) Lesser black-backed gull.
d) Black-headed gull.

Answers

Pages 26–27
1 The place where an organism lives.
2
a) Rabbit, squirrel, fox, bird, trees, grass, etc.
b) Pike, water lily, water boatman, duckweed, etc.
3
a) An organism has special features to help it to survive.
b) It has big ears to help it listen for foxes, and strong legs to help it to run away.
c) It has long stalks so its leaves reach the surface of the water.
4 Worms, earwigs, woodlice, etc. You would not find plants, because there is no light, and plants need light to grow.

Pages 28–29
1 Lettuce.
2 Slug, thrush, sparrowhawk.
3 Slug, thrush.
4 Thrush, sparrowhawk.
5 The direction the food goes through the chain.
6 Grass → cow → human.

Page 30
1 A micro-organism, or microbe.
2 Louis Pasteur.
3 Colds, flu, chicken pox, food poisoning.
4 Scurvy and heart disease.

Page 31
1 Brushing your teeth, and not eating sweets between meals.
2 Sneeze into a handkerchief.
3 You should have written down any three of the rules on page 31.
4 Raw meat still has microbes in it, which could get onto the cooked food, which will not be heated again before it is eaten.

Page 32
1 Micro-organisms feeding off food or dead organisms.
2 When it makes food go off.
3 It recycles nutrients (or it gets rid of dead things).

Page 33
1 You should have written down any four foods from the drawing on page 33.

2 It makes gas.
3 Sugar (food) and warmth.
4 It grows when it has food and warmth.

Pages 34–35
1
a) Transparent and hard.
b) Brittle.
2 It is absorbent and flexible.
3 It is strong and you can make it into different shapes.
4 Electricity does not go through plastic.
5 It is flexible, so you can make it into clothes, and heat does not travel through it easily.

Page 36
1 He used the same size squares, and the same amount of water each time.

Page 37
1 Degrees Celsius (or °C).
2 A thermometer.
3 23°C.

Page 38
1 Metal.
2 Any two of: wood, plastic, foam, trapped air.
3 There is lots of trapped air between the feathers, so a duvet is a good thermal insulator.

Page 39
1 One of: plastic, rubber, wood.
2 So electricity can flow through them.
3 Because electricity cannot flow through plastic, so you do not get a shock.

Pages 40–41
1 They may be covered by soil and grass, or by buildings or roads.
2 Bricks and concrete (if you have put wood, that is also correct!).
3 It lasts a long time and it looks nice.
4
a) Water can run through something.
b) Drop water on it and see if the water soaks in.
5 Granite, because it does not wear away. (Sandstone is also used in some places, even though it wears away easily, because it is easier to dig out of the ground.)

Page 42
1 Decaying plants and animals.
2 Clay soils.
3 Sandy soils (or chalky soils).

Page 43
1 Wood and metal (or anything else that is solid).
2 Water and honey (or any other liquid).
3 Any two of: sand, rice, flour, salt, sugar, etc.

Page 44
1 You can feel it when it is moving.
2 Oxygen, carbon dioxide, helium, natural gas.
3 You can squash a gas but you cannot squash a liquid. Gases spread out to fill a container, but liquids stay in the bottom of the container.
4 They change shape depending on the shape of the container they are in.

Page 45
1 Squeeze the sponge underwater, and you will see bubbles of air.
2 You can see bubbles of air if you pour water onto soil.
3 He used the same amount of soil each time, and started with the same amount of water.

Page 46
1 Solid, liquid and gas.
2 Cool it down to 0°C. (Freeze it.)
3 A gas turning into a liquid.
4 Evaporation happens at any temperature. Boiling only happens at 100°C.

Page 47
1 A liquid turning into a gas.
2 Spread out washing, so there is a bigger area for the water to evaporate from; heat the water (or clothes) to make the water evaporate faster; blow air over the clothes to carry away the evaporated water.

Answers

Page 48

1 A gas turning into a liquid, and the tiny drops of water formed on cold surfaces.
2 There is a lot of water vapour in the air (which has evaporated from hot water in the sink or shower).
3 Water vapour in the air condenses on the cold can.
4 On a warm day, the water vapour does not cool down enough to condense.

Page 49

1 100°C.
2 0°C.
3 100°C.

Pages 50–51

1 The sea, lakes, rivers and plants.
2 Water vapour condenses.
3 It runs into rivers and lakes, or soaks into the ground.
4 It is cleaned.
5 It is treated to make it safe before it is put into rivers or the sea.
6 Evaporating from the sea or a lake; condensing to make a cloud; freezing to make snow or hail; snow melting.

Pages 52–53

1 A container with lots of holes, which can be used to sort objects of different sizes.
2 The sand will go through the holes but the peas will not because they are too big.
3 Water will go through tiny holes in the paper, but the grains of sand are trapped because they are too big to go through the holes.
4 The sugar dissolves, and breaks into pieces that are small enough to fit through the holes in the filter paper.

Pages 54–55

1 Stir the water, use smaller pieces of sugar, use hot water.
2 Use more water.

3 The same amount of sugar, and the same kind of sugar each time. The same amount of water, and she should have stirred them all in the same way.

Page 56

1 The salt dissolves, so the pieces are small enough to go through the holes in the filter paper.
2 Let the water evaporate.
3 Trap the evaporated water and make it condense again.

Page 57

1 Any three of: melting, dissolving, condensing, freezing, evaporating.
2 Cooking food.

Pages 58–59

1 Concrete setting, and baking powder fizzing.
2 A new material (ash) is formed.
3 You should have written down two of the safety rules on page 59.
4 The heat melts the wax. Some of the melted wax evaporates, and some runs down the candle and becomes solid again. All these changes are reversible. Some of the wax burns, and this is an irreversible change.

Page 60

1
a) Two of: TV, computer, washing machine, or anything else that you have to plug in.
b) They need a lot of electricity.
2 Torches, personal stereos, mobile phones.
3 The electricity they provide is not powerful enough to harm you.
4 You should have written out five of the rules on page 60.

Page 61

1
a) Metals are good conductors of electricity.
b) Plastic is an insulator.
2
a) There is no battery.
b) The circuit is not complete – it needs another wire.

c) Both wires are connected to the same end of the battery.
d) There is a gap in the circuit.

Page 62

1 It has a voltage written on it.
2 Put more bulbs in (or use a battery with a lower voltage).
3 The bulbs might break.
4 Put another battery in so there is more electricity, or take a bulb out and join the wires up so the electricity does not have to be shared between the bulbs.

Page 63

1 It gets dimmer.
2 Thick wire.
3 Dimmer.
4 The length of the wire (and also the number of bulbs and batteries).

Page 64

1
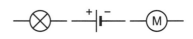

2 A closed switch
3
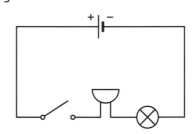

Page 65

1 Push away.
2 It is picking up more paper clips.
3 Iron and steel.
4 Use a magnet to try to pick up the cans. The steel cans are the ones that the magnet will pick up.

Page 66

1 Squash.
2 The spring pulls back.
3 A spring.
4 Newtons (N).

Answers

Page 67
1 A force that pulls everything towards the Earth.
2 The force of gravity pulling on something.
3 Hang it from a forcemeter.
4 Easier. Gravity is not as strong on the Moon, so the rock would have less weight than on Earth.

Page 68
1 A force that slows down moving objects.
2 Have a smooth surface.
3 Give it a smooth shape.
4 The tree has more area, so it has a larger air resistance.

Page 69
1 Your weight, and an upwards force from the floor.
2 The force from the dog is balanced by the force in its lead.

Page 70
1 An upwards force from water.
2
a) 25N
b) 2N
3) 6N

Page 71
1 Transparent means 'see through' and opaque means 'not see through'.
2

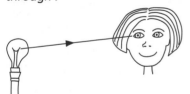

3 The stick is opaque, so light cannot go through it. Light travels in straight lines, so it cannot bend around the stick.

Page 72
1 The Earth is turning round on its axis and so the Sun seems to be in different places in the sky at different times of day.
2 A torch and two pieces of card.
3 Move the screen closer to the torch or move the other card further away from the torch.

Page 73
1 They reflect light from car headlights better, so it is easier for the driver to see you.
2 Your image.
3 Draw straight lines to show where the light goes.

Pages 74–75
1
a) The strings.
b) The skin.
2 How high or low a sound is.
3 Solids, liquids and gases.
4 Use soft materials like carpets and curtains.
5 To protect their ears from loud noises.
6 Because they are so far away that they would not be able to hear each other (or the noise of the engines would be too loud if they just tried talking).

Pages 76–77
1 Blow harder.
2 Hit it gently.
3 Move the slider out to make the air column longer.
4 Use a thicker string, a looser string, or a longer string.

Page 78
1
a) A sphere.
b) One from: photos from space, the bottom of ships disappears first when they sail away, ships can sail right around, or shadows are different lengths in different places.
2 Sun.
3 Moon.

Page 79
1 East.
2 The Earth is spinning.
3 24 hours (or one day).
4 The shadow is long and to the west of the stick in the morning. It gets shorter until midday, when it points north, and then gets longer again during the afternoon, and points further and further east.

Page 80
1 365$\frac{1}{4}$ days (or 1 year).
2 28 days.
3 It reflects light from the Sun.

Page 81
1
a) No, it depends on people's opinions. You can only investigate whether people think that flowers are pretty.
b) Yes – you can do an investigation to find out.
c) Yes – you can do an investigation to find out.
d) No – it depends on what the month is best for. You could investigate in which month flowers grow best, for instance, or which month people like best.

Page 82
1 Something you can change in an investigation.
2 One.
3 How much water it has, how much light it has, the temperature, the kind of soil, the size of pot.

Page 83
1
a) Ruler.
b) Centimetres (cm).
2
a) Measuring cylinder.
b) cm^3 (or ml).

Page 85
1
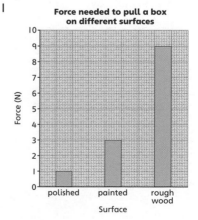

Page 86
1 Your graph should look like the one in the book.

Curriculum chart

Key Stage 2 Science Programme of Study	Qualifications and Curriculum Authority (QCA) Schemes of Work	Revision Guide Topic	Page
Sc1 Scientific enquiry			
1 Ideas and evidence in science *(1a, 1b)*	*Covered throughout Key Stage 2*	What makes you ill?	30
2 Investigative skills			
• *Planning (2a, 2b, 2c, 2d)*		Questions to investigate Fair tests	81 82
• *Obtaining and presenting evidence (2e, 2f, 2g, 2h)*		Measuring and units Tables Bar charts Line graphs	83 84 85 86
• *Considering evidence and evaluating (2i, 2j, 2k, 2l, 2m)*		Conclusions and evaluations	87

Sc2 Life processes and living things			
1 Life processes *(1a, 1b, 1c)*		Living things	5
2 Humans and other animals			
• *Nutrition (2a, 2b)*	3A *Teeth and eating* 5A *Keeping healthy*	Teeth A healthy diet	6 8
• *Circulation (2c, 2d)*	5A *Keeping healthy*	Your heart	12
• *Movement (2e)*	4A *Moving and growing*	Skeletons Muscles	10 11
• *Growth and reproduction (2f)*	5B *Life cycles*	The human life cycle	16
• *Health (2g, 2h)*	5A *Keeping healthy* 6B *Micro-organisms*	Health	14
3 Green plants			
• *Growth and nutrition (3a, 3b, 3c)*	3B *Helping plants grow well* 6A *Interdependence and adaptation*	Green plants Plants and soil	17 18
• *Reproduction (3d)*	5B *Life cycles*	Flowers Parts of a flower Pollination and fertilisation Seed dispersal Germination	19 20 21 22 23
4 Variation and classification *(4a, 4b, 4c)*	4A *Moving and growing* 4B *Habitats*	Sorting out living things	24
5 Living things in their environment *(5a)*			
• *Adaptation (5b, 5c)*	4B *Habitats* 6A *Interdependence and adaptation*	Habitats	26
• *Feeding relationships (5d, 5e)*	4B *Habitats* 6A *Interdependence and adaptation*	Feeding	28
• *Micro-organisms (5f)*	6B *Micro-organisms*	What makes you ill? Keeping healthy Decay Using micro-organisms to make food	30 31 32 33

Curriculum chart

Key Stage 2 Science Programme of Study	Qualifications and Curriculum Authority (QCA) Schemes of Work	Revision Guide Topic	Page
Sc3 Materials and their properties			
1 **Grouping and classifying materials** *(1a, 1b, 1c, 1d, 1e)*	3C *Characteristics of materials* 3D *Rocks and soils* 4C *Keeping warm* 4D *Solids and liquids* 4F *Circuits and conductors* 5C *Gases around us*	Materials and their uses Testing materials Hot and cold Conducting heat Conducting electricity Rocks Soils Solids and liquids Gases Investigating gases	34 36 37 38 39 40 42 43 44 45
2 **Changing materials** *(2a, 2b, 2c, 2d, 2e, 2f, 2g)*	4D *Solids and liquids* 5C *Gases around us* 5D *Changing state* 6C *More about dissolving* 6D *Reversible and irreversible changes*	Changing state Evaporation Condensation Melting and boiling The water cycle More about dissolving Reversible and irreversible changes Irreversible changes	46 47 48 49 50 54 57 58
3 **Separating mixtures of materials** *(3a, 3b, 3c, 3d, 3e)*	4D *Solids and liquids* 6C *More about dissolving*	Mixtures and filtering Separating solutions	52 56

Sc4 Physical processes			
1 **Electricity**			
• *Simple circuits (1a, 1b, 1c)*	4F *Circuits and conductors* 6G *Changing circuits*	Electricity – be safe! Electrical circuits Changing components Thin wires Drawing circuits	60 61 62 63 64
2 **Forces and motion**			
• *Types of force (2a, 2b, 2c, 2d, 2e)*	3E *Magnets and springs* 4E *Friction* 6E *Balanced and unbalanced forces*	Magnets and magnetic materials Springs Gravity and weight Friction Balanced forces Upthrust	65 66 67 68 69 70
3 **Light and sound**			
• *Everyday effects of light (2a, 2b, 2c)*	3F *Light and shadows* 6F *How we see things*	Light and seeing Changing shadows Reflecting light	71 72 73
• *Seeing (2d)*	3F *Light and shadows* 6F *How we see things*	Light and seeing	71
• *Vibration and sound (3e, 3f, 3g)*	5F *Changing sounds*	Sound and vibrations Pitch and loudness	74 76
4 **The Earth and beyond**			
• *The Sun, Earth and Moon (4a)*	5E *Earth, Sun and Moon*	Earth, Sun and Moon	78
• *Periodic changes (4b, 4c, 4d)*	3F *Light and shadows* 5E *Earth, Sun and Moon*	Day and night Orbits	79 80

Glossary

adapted	having features to help it to survive
balanced forces	forces that are the same size but in opposite directions
battery	part of a circuit that provides electricity
blood	red liquid that carries food around the bodies of humans and other animals
blood vessels	tubes that blood moves through (veins and arteries)
boiling	when a liquid is turning into a gas as fast as possible
burning	an irreversible change that gives out heat
carnivore	an animal that eats only other animals
circuit	a complete loop for electricity to flow around
components	parts of a circuit, such as batteries, bulbs and switches
conclusion	what you have found out in an investigation
condensation	a gas turning to a liquid, or the tiny drops of water that form on cold surfaces
conductor	something that lets heat or electricity flow through it
consumer	animals that eat plants or other animals
day	the time when it is light because our part of the Earth is facing the Sun
decay	what happens when micro-organisms feed off dead organisms, or off sugar and bits of food in your mouth
diet	the different foods that we eat
disperse	spread out, as when seeds are dispersed from the parent plant
dissolve	break up into very tiny pieces (e.g. in water)
drug	a substance that changes the way your body works
electricity	something that flows around a circuit, and makes things like TVs and light bulbs work
evaluation	deciding how good your investigation was
evaporation	when a liquid changes into a gas
factor	something that you can change in an investigation
fair test	an investigation where you only change one factor
fertilisation	when a pollen grain joins an ovum in a flower
fertiliser	a substance that adds nutrients to the soil
filter	paper with tiny holes in it that things like sand cannot pass through
flowers	the parts of a plant that help it to reproduce
food chain	a way of showing what eats what
forcemeter	an instrument containing a spring that is used to measure forces
freeze	a liquid changing to a solid
friction	a force that slows down moving objects
fruit	something that surrounds seeds, that animals like to eat
gas	a substance that is invisible, easy to squash, and spreads out to fill the container it is in
germination	when seeds start to grow
gravity	a force that pulls everything towards the Earth
habitat	the place where an organism lives
heart	pumps blood around the bodies of humans and other animals
herbivore	an animal that only eats plants
image	the picture of yourself that you can see in a mirror
insulator	something that does not let heat or electricity flow through it
irreversible change	a change that cannot be reversed, such as cooking food or burning
leaves	parts of a plant that make food using light, air and water
life cycle	the changes that happen to you as you get older
life process	things that all living organisms do, such as grow, move, take in food, use oxygen and reproduce
light source	something that gives out light, such as the Sun or a light bulb
liquid	a substance that is runny and cannot be squashed
magnet	something that can attract iron, and can attract or repel another magnet
magnetic material	a material like iron or steel that can be attracted by a magnet
mains electricity	powerful electricity that is supplied through sockets in the wall

Glossary

melt	when a solid changes to a liquid
micro-organisms	tiny organisms, sometimes called microbes or germs
mixture	different things jumbled up together
muscles	parts of your body that move your bones
nectar	a sweet liquid that flowers make to attract insects
newtons	the units used for measuring force and weight
night	when it is dark because our side of the Earth is facing away from the Sun
nutrients	substances that plants need to keep healthy
omnivore	an animal that eats plants and other animals
orbit	the path that the Earth takes around the Sun, or the Moon takes around the Earth
ova	the eggs in a flower (*singular, ovum*)
ovary	the part of a flower that contains the ova
ovum	one of the eggs that is in a flower (*plural, ova*)
petals	parts of a flower around the stamens and stigma – often brightly coloured to attract insects
photosynthesis	this is how plants make new materials to help them grow (using water, air and light)
pitch	how high or low a sound is
pollen	tiny grains made by the male parts of a flower
pollination	when pollen from one flower is taken to another flower
predator	an animal that kills other animals for food
prey	an animal that gets eaten by other animals
producer	any plant – plants make their own food from light, air and water
properties	what a material or substance is like
pulse	the movement of blood that you can feel in your neck or wrists
pulse rate	the number of heart beats per minute
reflection	when light bounces off a mirror
reproduction	making new animals or plants
respiration	this is how living things use oxygen to help them to use their food
reversible change	a change that can be made to go backwards, such as melting and freezing
roots	parts of a plant that hold it in the soil and take in water
seeds	parts of a plant that can grow into new plants
sepals	parts of a flower that protected it when it was a bud
shadow	a place where there is no light because light cannot travel through opaque materials
skeleton	all the bones in your body
soil	material made from bits of rock and decaying organisms
solid	a substance that is usually hard, keeps the same shape and is difficult to squash
solution	a mixture of water with something dissolved in it
stamens	the male parts of the flower that make pollen
state	whether something is a solid, a liquid or a gas
stem	supports a plant and contains tubes to carry water up the plant
stigma	the top of the female part of a flower
style	the female part of a flower that joins the ovary to the stigma
temperature	how hot or cold something is
upthrust	an upwards force from water
vibrate	move backwards and forwards quickly
water vapour	water when it is a gas
weight	the force of gravity pulling on something
year	the length of time it takes for the Earth to go around the Sun once

Index